How to be a
Happy
Homosexual
a guide for gay men

Terry Sanderson

The Other Way Press

Terry Sanderson is a Relate-trained counsellor and the author of several self-help books for gay men. He has also worked on the problem page at *Woman's Own* magazine and is a well-known journalist in the gay press.

How to be a Happy Homosexual was first published in 1986 and this fifth edition has been substantially re-written and updated to take into account the dramatic changes that have happened in gay life.

The Other Way Press
PO Box 130
London W5 1DQ
0181-998 1519 [from 22 April 2000: 020-8998 1519]
email .... otherway@dircon.co.uk
website .... www.otherway.dircon.co.uk

How to be a Happy Homosexual
© Terry Sanderson 1999

Fifth edition published 1999

British Library Cataloguing-in-Publication Data
A catalogue entry for this book is available from the British Library

ISBN: 0-948982-11-X

Printed by Biddles of Guildford

Distributed by Turnaround Publisher Services 0181-829 3000

Contents

To Keith

who helps me practise what I preach

Introduction

In 1969, on London's Hampstead Heath, a couple of hundred young people staged the first British Gay Pride March. It was one of the first public showings of the newly-formed Gay Liberation Front, an organisation whose ideas were to profoundly change gay life all over the world. Now, as we enter the twenty-first century, the efforts of those early pioneers have been rewarded in ways that they could only have dreamed about. But the road has been rocky and hard, and the journey is far from over.

In the years that have passed since those early efforts, lesbian and gay people have created a whole community for themselves. It is a community that can provide the support and encouragement that most of the wider society still refuses to give. It is a diverse community, widely-scattered and sometimes difficult to define, but, whatever our detractors say, it's a vibrant, creative community—and it is strong. The debate on our lives has pushed itself to the top of the social and political agenda.

Despite all this, prejudice and bigotry persists. Centuries of cruelty and ignorance will not be eliminated in a few decades, and our society's deep-rooted homophobia is only slowly being dismantled. Gay and lesbian children and young people are still denied the essential information that would help them feel comfortable with their feelings. They are refused encouragement and reassurance and instead are given disapproval and negative messages about themselves.

Society's refusal to accept that some children are going to grow up gay means that each generation of gay people reaches maturity carrying the message that their sexuality is inferior, undesirable and even corrupt. The very people from whom they need approval—parents, siblings, friends and work colleagues—often refuse to give it. Self-esteem can be deeply damaged at an early age, and it can take a long time to recover from such negative indoctrination. It is hard to be an outcast, and the temptation is for young people to stay in the closet. But the closet is a dark place, full of misery and self-denial. Far from being an escape route, it is a torture chamber. The pressures of the closet should not be underestimated, and the misery it induces should not be ignored. The number of young gay people who attempt suicide is tragically high. One survey of gay teenagers estimated that one in five had attempted to kill or seriously harm themselves.

While there is now more support within the gay community for the emerging gay person, it can still be a long, lonely journey to escape the closet, and a hard job to break down the door. People will tell you that being gay is a curse—"Why do you call yourself gay", they enquire, "when everyone knows that homosexuals are the most unhappy people in the world?" The idea that "gay" is an inappropriate word for homosexuals to have chosen for themselves—especially in the shadow of Aids—also begs a question for all people who define themselves as gay. How many of us still subscribe to the idea that homosexuals can't be happy?

There are many other "reasons" people invent to object to our existence, and they all serve to illustrate how deeply ingrained homophobia is in our society. Britain's notorious tabloid newspapers often reveal a crude and vicious contempt for gay people and the community we have created. The strength that homosexuals have discovered over the past few years has worried many people, and this fear has caused them to react by attacking the gay movement.

Yet despite the reactionary nature of many of our institutions, and the remorseless attempts by some sections of the press to humiliate and demean us, the gay community has never been stronger. As well as widespread homophobia, there is also plenty of liberal tolerance in this country, which makes it perfectly possible for gay men and women to be free from the fear and self-loathing that has marred the lives of so many in the past. And this tolerance is increasing, as opinion polls repeatedly show. A poll in the *Independent on Sunday* in December 1997 showed that "the percentage of people who believe that sexual relationships between men are wrong has fallen by more than a third during the past ten years. In 1987, 74 per cent though that sexual relations between men were 'always or mostly wrong'. This month the figure has fallen to 44 per cent in the survey of 1,442 people."

This slow, but sure, change in attitudes is a further reason why you should not deny yourself full expression as a gay person.

You still don't believe it can be done? It's already happening all over the country! An increasing number of gay men and women are claiming their right to a fulfilled emotional life. They face the same problems as anyone else—paying the rent, washing the dishes, sorting out the ups and downs of their relationships—but they identify themselves as homosexual, and live accordingly. They live without apology, and with a certain amount of pride. They do it in their own way. I am certainly not going to suggest that there is a "correct" formula for living a gay life, all I'm saying is that homosexuality doesn't have to dominate everything, just so long as you've taken the trouble to put it into its proper place. It's been proved over and over again that homosexuals can be happy, so long as they give themselves permission.

To pave the way to a contented gay lifestyle, you must be ready to make changes. This will be difficult at first, painful even. You may be stirring up feelings you've kept under wraps until now and there are likely to be confrontations that make your knees tremble. The end result, though, will be a freer, happier you. You will be freed from the control of other people's opinions and manipulations and your happiness will be the paramount motivation in your life.

Making Changes

Change is frightening. It means abandoning habits that give the illusion of security and an insulation from discomfort. These evasions block any opportunity for lasting happiness. It is time to embark on a new path, one that will ultimately lead to your happiness as a homosexual. It is a difficult road, fraught with obstacles and temporary upsets. It will lead you into unexplored areas of your life, scary places which you may have been trying hard to avoid. You will be engaged in this journey for the rest of your life, but it will bring its own invaluable rewards. And remember, the further you go, the easier it gets. The journey, however, will never be complete while you're alive.

That's the excitement of it, because this is a journey to the very core of your being. It is a trip that most heterosexuals will never have to take. They do not have to examine their inner selves in the same way, because their place in the world comes ready-made and guaranteed—so long as they follow the rules. For gay people, it's a journey without maps.

If you need further persuasion, think of the alternatives. You could spend the rest of your life hiding your homosexuality from others and, to an extent, yourself. This will mean long years of vigilance. You must be careful that no-one ever has an inkling of your true sexuality. You must be wary of ever having a satisfying and enriching love affair with someone of your own sex. It will mean a constant fear of your parents, friends and employers finding out about your "terrible secret". Eventually you will come to hate yourself, because for the rest of your life you will be reinforcing in your mind the idea that your sexuality is inferior and shameful. You will be sentencing yourself to an existence based on lies. Choose to be honest with yourself. This is, perhaps, the most important thing of all. Don't delude yourself that because all is tranquil on the surface, all is well within. Running away from the truth takes a lot of energy and it has a profoundly disturbing effect on the way you see yourself. Because there is constant pressure to be secretive—sometimes from other people, but often from ourselves—it is possible that the homosexual part of us becomes smothered and separated from the rest of our personality.

It's quite possible—even probable—that you'll reach old age emotionally unfulfilled, lonely and bitter.

Alternatively, you could realise that your homosexuality is a gift to be valued and enjoyed, one of the most important elements that goes to make up the essential you. It isn't everything, but then again, if you continue to deny it, it will cloud all corners of your life. You can express your sexuality with dignity, humour, friendship and love. You can be honest, truthful and strong. When you are unashamed of your sexuality you will lose your fear of other people finding out about it. If you like yourself, you will be able to resist the negative opinions of others. What they think about your sexuality will always be secondary to what you think about it yourself.

Seeking approval

Some gay men try to please everyone in a vain attempt to fend off awkward questions about their sexuality. The desire to be liked is basic to all of us, of course, but it should be kept in proportion. You can't be loved by everyone, however hard you try. Attempting to be the universal Mr Nice Guy (which is what many gay men do) means sacrificing the true, probably more interesting, you.

Ironically, constant pandering to those from whom you seek approval will only result in their losing respect for you. The more you try to please those you fear, the greater will be their power over you.

Have you noticed that those who are liked most are those with the liveliest minds, the people who aren't afraid to harbour contradictory opinions and aren't afraid to answer back? People who are true to themselves are often the ones who are sought out for friendship. "Yes-people" are despised by all.

The fear is that if people know you are homosexual, they will hate you. They might; but the likelihood is that they will not. They can just as easily go on liking you; it doesn't take any more effort and they have little to gain by pushing you away. You will find that most people who are close to you will accept the news with equanimity. They may even feel flattered that you have chosen to share this most intimate part of yourself with them.

It is a constantly reassuring contradiction in human nature that people who say they "can't stand homosexuals" are often supportive of individual gay people. It's easy to hate an anonymous group, especially when they have been characterised as "evil" and "immoral" for many centuries, but not so easy to hate individuals who you like, or even love. So, in the face of society's disapproval, friends and family may be perfectly able to accept each gay person on his or her own merits.

In my many years of counselling homosexuals, the saddest aspect has been the cry from some older gay people that they have "wasted" their lives. However materially successful they have been, and whatever their achievements in their chosen field, they have denied themselves the comfort and satisfaction of human love, simply so they wouldn't be rejected by the society they so wanted to please. In their youth, of course, there was every possibility that they would have paid an enormous penalty for being honest. Before 1967, a declaration of homosexuality would have carried legal and social consequences which we can hardly imagine today. This is sufficient to explain the choice they made— nobody wants to be a martyr or an outcast. (Read Quentin Crisp's book *The Naked Civil Servant* to get some idea of what the repercussions of Coming Out were only a few short decades ago, or try to see the film *Victim*, starring Dirk Bogarde, which vividly illustrates the misery of gay life in the Forties and Fifties.)

The injustice and prejudice that still exists today is not on the same scale. There may be some repercussions from Coming Out, but they are much less likely to be as catastrophic as they might have been a couple of generations ago. Don't make them excuses for inaction.

Your life is yours and yours alone, and no-one should have more authority over it than you. If you allow others to take control, you are inviting unhappiness and frustration. When you hand over your decisions to others you also hand over your potential for joy and growth.

The relentless campaign of misinformation put out by the straight press has tried to damage the progress being made by gay people. But this has, in the main, failed, and is no longer a reason to consider staying in the closet. The British tabloid press has become a music-hall joke. If someone wants to insult a piece of journalism they say "That's worthy of *The Sun*". The popular press has repeatedly been shown to be dishonest, unreliable, politically partisan and often just plain malicious. Why should we allow such worthless attacks to dictate the direction of our lives?

Now, more than ever before, it is important for you as an individual, and for all of us as a community, to make ourselves known. As the late Brian Kennedy wrote in *City Limits* magazine: "Ultimately lesbians and gay men possess a secret weapon which can out-manoeuvre both government and press propaganda, if we choose to use it. If every lesbian or gay man was open about their lives with a dozen or so heterosexuals that we know, we could transform public debate on the issue. All the indications are that the public are widely ignorant rather than fundamentally bigoted, and an encounter with an openly gay person can change perspectives. Unfortunately, the flipside of this tactic is that our closetry, the times we cover or hide our lifestyle, is probably the greatest asset available to our enemies. The personal choices we make now between openness and the closet may well determine the shape of gay life into the next century."

The slogan from the early days of the gay movement "The personal is political" is still relevant today. For, as you struggle to make your own life more open, more enjoyable and free from fear, you are helping those of your fellow gays still in isolation, and the generations that will follow.

As we fight our great battle for liberation, acceptance and equality—personal and communal—we can enlist the support of our families and friends. It's there if you ask for it, whatever our detractors might say. We have a place in the world on our own terms and we have to demand that it is respected.

Aids is a serious complication in our lives which needs to be faced. The gay community has risen to the challenge and the effort at loosening the grip of this virus on our future has been heroic. In the Western world at least, medical developments have made Aids a manageable illness for many. There is as yet no cure, but HIV infection is no longer the automatic death-sentence it once was. All the same, we cannot be complacent. HIV is an adaptable virus. It has outwitted "miracle" drugs before. We must keep up our guard.

The last decade has produced many examples of courage and determination. Together, we can slay the twin monsters of intolerance and disease.

No special knowledge needed

Those who have already taken the step to free themselves are not heroes: they are simply people who have found the burden of denial intolerable. They are no more courageous than you or I, it is simply that they have made the decision to move on to better things.

And so can you!

There is nothing superhuman about the people who have asserted their right to have a life of their own definition. They come from all age groups and all walks of life, from every class and culture. They made a decision and acted upon it; now it can be your turn.

Once you've made that decision, happiness is within reach.

1. *Getting to like yourself*

People who are homosexual generally start out with a very poor opinion of themselves. How could it be otherwise? We are programmed at a very early age with the idea that homosexuality is mad, bad, sad or tragic. Our friends at school reserve words like "poof", "queer" and, "faggot" as their most cutting insults. Our parents warn us to beware of "people like that" and any sex education we might have is likely to omit all mention of homosexuality—or mention it only in connection with disease and death. Disapproval seems all around. No wonder, then, that so many gay people have such a hard time liking themselves.

In this chapter we will look at some of the techniques you can use to unburden yourself of this negative conditioning.

Coming out to yourself
Challenging long-held values is enormously difficult and even more so when there is little apparent encouragement to do so. But it is possible. We are going to start the re-learning process and counter some of the damaging things that are said about us.

But before this can be done successfully, we have to "come out" to ourselves. Acknowledging our homosexuality, even silently, is not always as easy as it sounds. Many gay people are, of course, aware of their unconventional sexuality long before they know there is a word to describe it. They will say "I was born this way" or "I've been gay ever since I can remember." Others come to the realisation later in life— sometimes very much later. I once counselled a man of ninety-three who said he'd held his homosexuality "in abeyance" since the First World War. He had been in love with another soldier, but his lover had been killed on the Somme. Gordon returned home, married and became a father. He lived a conventional family life until the late 1970s when his wife died. Then Gordon decided to "come out" in the very last year of his long life. This might seem like an extreme example, but it illustrates how persistent can be the need to give expression to these basic feelings. They chased Gordon over the best part of a century and eventually caught up with him. Gordon came out to his son—who was sixty-eight years old himself!

So successful is the pressure to dislike ourselves that many women and men resist their homosexual feelings completely until they reach their thirties or forties. Eventually they can suppress them no longer and the acknowledgement at this late date can be particularly distressing if it leads to the break-up of marriages and families.

Sometimes people define themselves as bisexual, which means they feel capable of relating erotically to members of both sexes. Indeed, it has been said that most of us are bisexual and that exclusive homosexuality and exclusive heterosexuality are the extreme ends of the sexual spectrum. How you choose to define yourself, if at all, is entirely up to you.

Others think they may be gay because their relationships with the opposite sex have been strained and unsuccessful. If you read the problem pages in magazines you will have seen this idea popping up repeatedly. "I've tried to go out with girls but it never works," goes the young man's plea. "I feel such a failure because I really would like a girlfriend, but I never know what to do and they just laugh at me. Do you think I could be gay?"

The real problem for young men who think like this is probably not gayness at all, but simply ineptitude in relating to the opposite sex. If you're straight, and not having a very good time, you may think that life in the gay world would be simpler. Think again. Equally, those gays who think "passing for straight" is a way of escaping the hassle that goes with their sexuality should realise that they, too, are storing up trouble for later life.

The awareness of what is our true sexuality might dawn slowly or it might be as certain as the sunrise. Whichever, it has to be clear in our own mind before we can make progress. This book is for those who think of themselves primarily as gay and want to accept homosexuality as their true orientation.

Exploding some myths

There are several widespread myths about homosexuality and homosexual people, which persist despite efforts to counter them. You should think through the issues that lie behind the myths and be ready to challenge them when they inevitably crop up. Knowledge is your best ally: read about the issues and find out the truth; contact one of the gay book shops listed at the back of this book for their reading lists.

Myth one: "All gay men are effeminate"

The most common stereotype of gay men is the limp-wristed, mincing weed. This is the shorthand used by some lazy cartoonists and comedians to suggest homosexuality (together with the moustachioed leather queen). Even for the most hardened bigot, it is becoming harder to sustain this myth. As more and more gay men come out, their diversity becomes more apparent. And yet still some heterosexuals seem surprised when they discover that even some of Hollywood's toughest and sexiest screen heroes have been homosexual. Indeed, when it was revealed that Rock Hudson was gay, America reeled in astonishment. A similar frisson went through Britain's establishment when the country's leading Shakespearean actor, Ian McKellen, decided to reveal to the world that he was gay. Here was a man who had played some of literature's most masculine and romantic heroes, and done so very convincingly. Those who had been enthralled by his magnetic sexual appeal on stage were bewildered when they realised that it did not emanate from heterosexual feelings at all. It caused many people to reappraise their ideas of what a gay man is. Other gay men to have come out in recent years include the entertainer Michael Barrymore, singer George Michael and at least seven MPs.

This is not to say there aren't any effeminate gay men. There are. There are also effeminate straight men, who must find life very difficult, cast as they are into entirely inappropriate roles. Sometimes called "camps" or "femmes" or "queens", effeminate homosexuals are the most easily identifiable members of our community. They are the ones who take the brunt of the violence and hate that is directed at us. Most are not using effeminacy as an affectation, it's simply the way they are. However, once on the gay scene such people may exaggerate their mannerisms and play up to their image. "Camping it up" in gay company can be great fun, and a great release of tension. If you consider yourself to be effeminate, you'll generally find acceptance within the gay community.

Some straight women seem less threatened by camp men and many effeminate gays have found a comfortable niche in mainly female environments. Other effeminate gay men find that they can, through charm and force of personality, overcome people's initial reactions to them and become respected and liked in other fields, too.

But effeminate men do not have to relegate themselves to the role of eccentric or clown. The whole gamut of human experience is available to those who will take it. It isn't necessary to limit yourself because of other people's perception. Those who are effeminate have probably suffered a lifetime of having their mannerisms and speech patterns pointed out to them. I have spoken to many effeminate gay men who tell horrendous stories of persecution at school, at work and in the street. It takes courage for them to maintain a reasonable level of self-esteem, especially when they are being constantly hounded. Hopefully, some of what is written in this book will be helpful to those who feel limited by their so-called effeminacy. Defiance does not always have to take the form of flaunting it. You can decide to live a conventional life if that is what you want, learning to cope assertively with other people's ignorant and prejudiced reactions. For anyone who feels that a more assertive approach to life would help them cope better, there are numerous books and courses to help.

Myth two: "All gay men are child molesters"

This myth is very widely believed, despite overwhelming evidence to the contrary. It confuses homosexuality with paedophilia, a sexual attraction to children. In fact it has been shown repeatedly that something like 98% of sexual assaults on children have been committed by heterosexual men upon young girls. And most of these attacks occur within the victim's own family.

Even so, it is gay men who are perceived as the danger to children, either because they are seen as potential rapists or that they have some mysterious "influence" on youthful minds. An illustration of this was contained in an article in *The Independent on Sunday*, when a member of the Conservative Family Campaign was quoted as saying: "Homosexuals always want new recruits because homosexuality is not something you're born with, it's acquired behaviour...they're trying to indoctrinate and corrupt young children."

You should never allow yourself to assume feelings of guilt when you read newspaper reports of homosexual assaults on young boys—these, too, are perpetrated often by nominally heterosexual men. Two wrongs do not make a right, of course, and sometimes gay men *are* paedophiles. That does not mean that you are guilty, too. I do not see all heterosexual men assuming the guilt for the actions of the minority who are child abusers. Neither should we.

Myth 3: "Homosexuals are really women trapped in men's bodies"

Once again, gay men are confused with something else entirely. This time it's transsexuals—people who believe that they have been born into the wrong gender. Many transsexuals eventually have a surgical operation to change their sex; most never consider themselves to be gay at any stage in their life.

Myth 4: "Gay men love dressing up as women"

Some do, and drag queens are very popular as cabaret performers in gay clubs and pubs, but they are a small minority within a minority. Transvestism—as dressing up in the clothes of the opposite sex is called—is something that an awful lot of straight men like to do, too!

I've never come across a satisfactory explanation as to why so many heterosexual men like to wear women's clothing — some say it is because they want to get closer to women, not that they want to *be* women. This was one of the commonest problems I came across when I worked on the problem page of a woman's magazine. Wives just couldn't understand why their husbands wanted to wear their clothes, but many of them came to see that it was just another expression of sexuality and indulged their husband's little kink. After all, no-one was ever harmed by wearing a frock—ask your mother!

In the gay world few people turn a hair at cross-dressing.

Myth 5: "Gays are responsible for Aids"

Usually followed by "... and they're spreading it to innocent people." Such thinking is highly insulting and shot through with ignorance. Who do the hijackers of the "moral high ground" consider to be the "innocent victims" of Aids and who, by implication, do they think are "guilty"? It doesn't take a genius to work that one out. Or, as one commentator, Geoffrey Levy, in the *Daily Mail* put it: "In the West, Aids always has been and always will be a disease primarily contracted by, and circulated among, practising, promiscuous homosexuals." This may be technically correct in Britain at present, but there is no guarantee that it will remain that way. Heterosexuals cannot afford to be complacent about how the Aids epidemic will develop. They cannot afford to imagine that their heterosexuality gives them some kind of automatic protection. And it is verging on the criminal for journalists to encourage this complacency.

However, the myth persists—Aids is a "gay disease", and homosexuals are responsible for its genesis and spread. But Aids is caused by a virus and it survives by invading human hosts. It does not care whether those hosts are straight or gay, just so long as it can get into their bloodstream. It is unfortunate that a particular sexual activity practised by some homosexual men, namely anal intercourse, is an efficient transmitter of the virus. In other parts of the world, vaginal intercourse is a major route of infection. And so we find that on a global scale Aids is a disease that affects mainly heterosexuals. Of the millions of cases that now exist, more than 75% are a result of heterosexual intercourse. We know that there are other factors at work in the developing world that do not apply in the rich and well-nourished West.

Loaded words such as "promiscuous" are misleading in this context. Homosexuals do not have a monopoly on promiscuity. After all, the most famous multiple lovers have all been heterosexual: Don Juan, Casanova, the Marquis de Sade, all bywords for sexual excess. And all straight. Having more than one partner does not necessarily put people at risk of acquiring HIV; so long as they practise safer sex all the time, they could have a hundred partners and not be at any significant risk.

The transmission of HIV is not necessarily connected to "promiscuity", it is connected chiefly with anal intercourse, and you could find yourself infected with HIV after experiencing that only once.

The idea that we have brought this epidemic upon ourselves through "self-indulgence" is nonsense. Homosexuals, like other people, need love and affection. We want relationships and intimacy in the same way as the rest of the human race. It is not "indulgent" to want to love each other. Stupid comparisons with cigarette smoking and excessive drinking are crude, simplistic and fatuous. Wanting to be loved is not the same as being addicted to tobacco.

Find out as much as you can about the syndrome so that you are ready to counter these ignorant and oft-repeated myths. For our own safety we must all become experts in this ghastly peril. Read the chapter on gay health and keep up to date with developments and discoveries through the gay press and the responsible straight media. Medical research continues apace in the Western world, and recent pharmaceutical developments are transforming Aids into a manageable condition that is no longer inevitably fatal.

Myth 6: "Gay relationships never last, and all gays end up lonely"

This may well once have had an element of truth. In previous generations the legal penalties for being caught engaged in homosexual activities, however discreet and private, were so swingeing that to enter into an open homosexual relationship was tantamount to inviting a prison sentence. It was not the "nature" of gay relationships that caused them to be transitory and fraught, it was the outside pressures. Many people, including some gays, cling to the idea that two people of the same sex cannot achieve any kind of stability in a relationship because their sexuality rules against it. "Gays are naturally promiscuous", they'll say, suggesting that all homosexuals behave in the same way in all circumstances, which is patently ridiculous. However, even though they don't stand up to close examination, generalisations of this kind are very useful to the anti-gay myth-makers. Thousands of gay couples have proved that long-term, dignified and committed relationships are perfectly possible. If that is what you are looking for, then rest assured that it can be done.

Equally, there is no commandment carved in stone that says you must have a monogamous relationship. The choice is yours. Just make sure it is an informed and willingly undertaken choice.

Myth 7: "Homosexuals proselytise in order to gain new converts"

Proselytising is defined in *The Oxford English Dictionary* as "converting from one opinion to another". Presumably, those people who accuse gays of proselytising mean that we attempt to change heterosexuals into homosexuals. How this is achieved is never made clear by the proponents of this argument. However, it is still a widely believed myth, and provided the starting point for the now-infamous Section 28 of the Local Government Act, 1988. This Section forbids the "promotion of homosexuality" in schools run by local authorities in England and Wales.

When it was introduced into Parliament, many of its supporters asserted that young people were being "taught homosexuality" in their classrooms. Many said that such teaching "corrupted" young minds and encouraged homosexual experimentation. Fortunately a more enlightened era is upon us, and there are high hopes that Section 28 will eventually be abolished.

However, the people who hold to the opinion that gay people seek to "indoctrinate" children never explain exactly what they imagine goes on in sex education lessons which cover the facts about homosexuality. In their terms, it seems that merely mentioning the word is sufficient for children to be immediately "converted" from potential heterosexuals into "confirmed homosexuals". They must imagine that heterosexuality is very unappealing if children can be turned off it so easily.

There is also some misunderstanding over the supposed "homosexual phase" in adolescence. This is another favourite of the myth-makers. The theory was given this airing in the *Sunday Times* by Mr A. Scammell, a consultant paediatrician: "A proportion of boys are starting physical changes of puberty at fourteen and fifteen. It is only when these changes occur that the full realisation of what sexuality is about can dawn on an individual. The mental adjustment to puberty is a major psychological stress in most people, and for many there is confusion about sexual attraction: attraction to the same sex and the opposite sex are very common at this stage."

We have to remember that doctors can be as homophobic as anyone else. Mr Scammell offers no evidence for his hypothesis, and there are hundreds of gay men who would be prepared to come forward and directly contradict it. Many homosexuals—and I count myself in this number—knew that they were homosexual in early childhood, long before they reached puberty. I have spoken to scores of men who insist that they were aware of their sexuality before they even knew it had a name, or that it was socially unacceptable.

In reality, the "homosexual phase" usually consists of little more than a crush on the teacher, or some other admired figure, and perhaps a bit of exploratory fumbling behind the bike sheds. This is just youthful curiosity for those who will go on to become heterosexual, but important for those who will be gay. Far from "damaging" young people, a little bit of sexual exploration with their peers can help them work out for themselves which place they will occupy on the sexual spectrum. This is a far cry from the "exploitation" and "coercion" which is trumpeted by the myth-makers.

Persuading people to change their sexual orientation is not something that is so easily achieved. Psychiatrists have been trying to perfect ways of changing homosexuals into heterosexuals for many years, with little or no success—and that was even when the subject wanted to change. How the process is to be achieved the other way round, when the person supposedly being converted is unwilling to change, is still the secret of those who say it is possible.

The probable truth is that people who define themselves as heterosexual occasionally experiment with homosexuality. They might do it because there is no-one of the opposite sex to relate to—in prison, or the army for instance—or it may be that they have become attracted to one particular individual whom they admire, are fond of and with whom they wish to become more intimate. Human feelings are not regulated by the arbitrary rules of the "moralists". Someone who is a notional heterosexual might turn to homosexuality for any number of reasons and vice versa. That choice should be respected as their own.

Myth 8: "Gay relationships are sterile because homosexuals can't have children"

Who says they can't? Homosexuals have the same physiological construction as heterosexuals and so there is no reason why they should not have children if they want them. Many homosexuals have been married and are parents already. Some gay people have had children of their own through a variety of arrangements such as artificial insemination and surrogacy.

Many other gay people don't want children, just as many heterosexual couples opt for a childless partnership. The relationship is not automatically valueless just because there are no children in it. Indeed, it could be argued that such people are contributing to the good of mankind by refusing to add to an already overcrowded planet. It has been noted many times that gay people without children have often directed the energy that they might have expended on child-rearing into other humanitarian or artistic endeavours that have benefited the whole of mankind.

Child-rearing for some people is a wonderful experience, and anyone who has an overwhelming desire to be a parent should not feel that they are precluded because they are gay. The idea that children will be emotionally damaged if they are not raised in a mixed-sex family has been disproved repeatedly, so neither should this be a reason for denying yourself parenthood. Our opponents might be convinced that anything other than conventional male-female partnership can be nothing but a "pretend family relationship", but hundreds of couples have proved them wrong.

Some progressive local authorities in Britain have approved policies which, in theory, allow gay people to foster or adopt children on the same basis as heterosexuals. This has happened occasionally, although several cases have been gratuitously and sensationally "exposed" in trashy tabloid newspapers, making it more difficult for authorities to take the risk of fostering to gay couples.

If the desire for parenthood is an overwhelming ambition in your life, and you really are determined to achieve it, there are ways of overcoming the difficulties. There are support groups for gay parents, where positive role models and shared experience can lessen the isolation. Find them listed in *Gay Times* magazine.

Myth 9: "Homosexuals have chosen to be gay, so it follows they can choose not to be"

The anti-gay myth-makers love this one. The theory that homosexuality is a learned behaviour (and therefore, by implication, you can unlearn it) is comforting to those people who are bewildered and uncomfortable with gay sexuality. How reassuring it is to them to think that gay people are just doing it to be perverse.

There are several small religious organisations which claim that they can "counsel and pray" people out of their homosexuality. They base their theory on literal interpretations of the Bible which to a rational mind seem idiotic and childish. Such fundamentalists push their theory so enthusiastically because if the alternative turns out to be true—i.e. that homosexuality is the result of genetic factors and not immoral choice-making—then the Bible must have it wrong and the church has been persecuting homosexuals for two thousand years for something over which they have no control. Among organisations pushing this "cure" are Exodus, The True Freedom Trust, Living Waters and Pilot. If you come across them, give them a wide berth. That's if you value your peace of mind.

Nobody knows for certain why some people are gay and some aren't, but there have been several recent studies which seem to point in the direction of a strong genetic link. One American scientist discovered that there was a minute difference in the structure of the hypothalamus in homosexual men when compared to the heterosexual equivalent. Another

US scientist studied pairs of twins separated at birth, and found that even though they were not raised together, identical twins (being genetically identical) are far more likely to be both gay than non-identical twins.

The conclusion seems to be that there is probably a strong genetic factor involved in determining whether or not someone is gay. There are also probably other factors involved which as yet are unidentified.

This means that those people who cling to the idea that homosexuality is "caused by the way people are raised" or that sexual orientation is a matter of choice, and try to invent methods for "curing" gayness, are inflicting great cruelty. If you come across anyone offering a "cure" for homosexuality, approach them with caution—or better still, run a mile.

If you want to find out more about he research into a genetic predisposition to homosexuality, read "A Separate Creation—how biology makes us gay" by Chandler Burr (Bantam Books).

Demolishing the myths

Despite the growing evidence that homosexuality is a perfectly natural phenomenon, there are those who cannot let the matter rest. Moralisers, most of them religious, the press and a minority of "dinosaur" psychiatrists, often have adverse opinions about homosexuals and don't hesitate to express them. They constantly tell us things that we know from our own experience are not true. These "experts" have done immeasurable harm to the minds of countless homosexual people, and their irrational disapproval continues to torment particularly those gays who are alone and unsupported. Unless we get into the habit of rejecting these illogical and distorted representations of our lives, it is possible that they will start to erode our self-confidence.

Our recognising that we are surrounded by irrational negative messages about ourselves (some of them cunningly disguised) is the first step towards counteracting them. The way to a better self-image begins with the ability to contradict and disagree with the nonsense frequently written and spoken about homosexuality. We need to prime our critical faculties and start to look at the arguments with a more discriminating eye.

We'll now examine a few of the areas where the damage is done.

Not an illness

A few years ago when homosexuality was completely illegal and seen as a serious moral flaw, psychiatrists said that the only hope for homosexuals was a complete change of sexual orientation. To facilitate this, a technique called Aversion Therapy was employed. The idea was to put gay people off their sexual preferences by showing them erotic pictures of their own sex while administering electric shocks or emetics. The aim was to turn the "patient" to heterosexuality by creating an association between homosexual feelings and unpleasant sensations. This would cause the "patient" to turn to heterosexuality for his or her satisfaction.

The result of this cruel treatment was that the victim's sexual interest disappeared completely—until the "therapy" was over, when it returned in its homosexual form as before. The only change was that the gay person then felt even worse about his homosexuality. Admitting eventually that this did not work, the psychiatrists sat down for a rethink.

In the meantime, social attitudes were changing. Certain aspects of homosexual behaviour were decriminalised and the gay movement emerged. Public opinion shifted to a more tolerant stance. Psychiatrists, ever anxious to reflect the changing tide, began to say that homosexuals would be better off if they could "come to terms" with their sexuality and be "integrated into society"—the opposite, in fact, to what they had been saying a few years earlier.

Given the confusion and disagreement within the psychiatric profession about homosexuality, is there any reason for us to take any notice of what they say? Do they, in fact, know any more about the subject than we do ourselves? It seems they know considerably less. I doubt, though, whether all of them will relinquish their search for a "cause" and "cure" for homosexuality.

It has to be accepted that psychiatrists play an important part in the treatment of mental illness. But homosexuality is not a mental illness and, unless there are good reasons for it, homosexuals should resist the pressure, from whatever source, to "have treatment". The American Psychiatric Association removed homosexuality from their list of disorders in 1973.

It ain't necessarily so

The arguments of people who try to make homosexuality into a grave moral issue should be resisted. Homosexuality itself is not the problem, it is neither moral nor immoral. As with any form of conduct, it is how we behave that counts.

For instance, when a child is reported to have been assaulted by "a homosexual", the reaction is often to condemn homosexuality. But if a heterosexual commits a similar crime, his heterosexuality is not mentioned; no-one dares to suggest that it is heterosexuality itself that leads to such actions and that all heterosexuals should, therefore, be labelled "child molesters". Each individual with a sound mind is responsible for his or her own actions and you should strenuously resist taking on board any guilt feelings which these blanket condemnations of homosexuality are intended to induce.

"Ah," say the moralists, "but you see, it isn't homosexuals we condemn, it is the practice of homosexuality."

What this means, shorn of its righteousness, is that these people want us to live apart from each other and deny ourselves the love, sex and companionship they take for granted. Such thinking is almost breathtaking in its selfishness.

Recent discussion on homosexuality within the churches has rested almost entirely on this concept of "love the sinner, but hate the sin." Fundamentalists within the religious community have promulgated the idea that because there are biblical prohibitions against homosexuality, then all expression of homosexuality, however loving and respectful, is "sin".

These people use the Bible selectively, of course, and like secular politicians who see homosexuals as easy targets for vilification, the church has tried to use us a means of promoting their own interests. Ruthless evangelists, motivated more by greed than by truth, have sought to exploit the Aids crisis as a vehicle for their never-ending anti-gay venom. Particularly in America, these people have been shown repeatedly to be bare-faced liars and hypocrites. They have cheated the gullible and created hatred where there need have been none.

In Britain the churches wrangle endlessly over what they claim their particular God wants in regard to homosexuals. Often the arguments put forward are crude and lacking in humanity. This is evident even within the Anglican church, which many regard as the most moderate. The Church of England commissioned a report on sexuality from the House of Bishops which was published in 1991. In it the Bishops say that they cannot accept that homosexuality is as valid as heterosexuality, but that gay Christians have a right to express their sexuality in line with Christian teaching (that is, with good conscience, in non-exploitative ways that aim for faithfulness with one partner). This is how they put it:

> "Homosexual people are in every way as valuable to and as valued by God as heterosexual people. God loves us all alike, and has for each of us a range of possibilities within his design for the universe. This includes those who, for whatever reason, find themselves with a homophile orientation which, so far as anyone at present can tell, cannot in their case be changed, and within which therefore they have the responsibility of living human life creatively and well. Every human being has a unique potential for Christlikeness, and an individual contribution to make through that likeness to the final consummation of all things. Of Christian

homophiles some are clear that the way they must follow to fulfil this calling is to witness to God's general will for human sexuality by a life of abstinence. In the power of the Holy Spirit and out of love for Christ they embrace the self-denial involved, gladly and trustfully opening themselves up to the power of God's grace to order and fulfil their personalities within this way of life. This is a path of great faithfulness, travelled often under the weight of a heavy cross. It is deserving of all praise and the support of Church members through prayer, understanding and active friendship.

At the same time there are others who are conscientiously convinced that this way of abstinence is not the best for them, and they have more hope in growing in love for God and neighbour with the help of a loving and faithful homophile partnership, in intention lifelong, where mutual self-giving includes the physical expression of their attachment...We stand alongside them in the fellowship of the Church, all alike dependent on the undeserved grace of God."

This applies only to lay people and not to gay clergy, who the bishops say must remain celibate. However, in the summer of 1998, at the Lambeth Conference (which takes place every ten years, and involves the whole of the Anglican communion from all around the world), a resolution was passed which appeared to take a much harder line, and it was supported by the Archbishop of Canterbury. This shows that we cannot take for granted that our progress to acceptance and equality will be either smooth, or always in a forward direction.

Some religious leaders can still wield great influence over our lives, but that does not mean they are always right. Keep those critical faculties tuned and don't be afraid to confront authority when it talks nonsense. Some churches, of course, see no objections to loving homosexual relationships and believe that acceptance and love should prevail over hatred and intolerance.

If you have strong religious leanings which you see as being in conflict with your homosexuality, then you should contact one of the many gay religious groups. They'll help you see the whole thing from a different, much more positive, perspective. They'll help you work through the conflicts that cause so much unhappiness.

In the end, though, it is up to you to see your gayness not as an abiding evil but simply a different way of expressing your sexuality. Your conscience will tell you that you can love someone of your own sex without harming yourself or anyone else. And knowing it from the heart is worth a thousand theories and dogmas.

When considering these matters you have to ask yourself constantly whose opinion of your life is more important—theirs or yours? Trust yourself and you'll be free of the fear of disapproval.

If the religious arguments seem irrelevant or cruel, there is another approach which relies on the power of human good, rather than the supernatural. Humanism can give you a new way of looking at the world. Humanists believe it is possible to lead an ethical and good life without religion. The Gay and Lesbian Humanist Association (GALHA) is prominent within the gay community. Their address is at the back of the book.

But it's there in black and white

When statements are made in print, they take on an authority which is sometimes difficult to resist. However, a more critical approach to what is published in newspapers and magazines (and in some books) is an essential skill for gays. It is important for us to constantly challenge the misinformation and distortion we see about ourselves in print.

The isolated homosexual, who has no support, is unlikely to be cheered by what he or she reads in the popular press. None of Britain's tabloid newspapers will report matters of concern to homosexual people in a balanced way. In the case of Aids, it was the popular press that fanned the hysteria which attended early discussion of the disease. With a relish that was alarming to behold, the British press encouraged a climate of fear that has taken a long time to diminish.

The behaviour of the press over the Aids issue, over gays in the churches, over the struggle for an equal age of consent, has given us new insights into the way anti-gay feeling can be manipulated by a hostile media. There is little doubt that some of the tabloid press has declared war on homosexuals in Britain, and it's up to us to fight back with all means we have at our disposal.

Of course, it could be said that we are blaming the messenger for an unpalatable message, namely that Britain is an extremely homophobic nation. (The 1994 British Social Attitudes Survey found that 64% of those questioned thought that homosexuality was "wrong"—in 1987 the figure was 74%.) The newspapers would claim that they are simply reflecting their readers' opinions in carrying such aggressive and insulting journalism about gay people. There may well be an element of truth in this, but the hostility goes well beyond any reasonable bounds. The use of abusive and insulting language, and of distortion and lies in relation to homosexuality is still quite common.

Broadsheet newspapers, on the other hand, at least treat the matter seriously. Some of these, too, are hostile but the more liberally-inclined have been supportive when reporting events which affect us. Increasingly, gay voices are being heard in the pages of these papers. Homosexuality—at least in the pages of *The Guardian* and *Independent*—is no longer treated as the shock/horror subject it once was.

Always analyse carefully anything you read about homosexuality in the newspapers, and don't take any story at face value. Over and over again the press has been caught out lying and distorting the facts. Never before have newspapers been so distrusted and disliked. The malevolent tabloid newspapers have become a blot on our society trying, as they do, to cause harm to gay people and other minorities of which they disapprove, for political or other motives.

The power of contradiction

When you have begun to feel more secure in the liberty brought by coming out, and you truly believe that you are the sole authority on your feelings, then you might like to reinforce your convictions by actually arguing with your detractors. This is an excellent way of sorting out what you really think about issues and also of increasing self-esteem.

You could start with a letter to the editor of your local paper when something anti-gay is printed, or perhaps a personal letter to a public figure who has said something offensive about homosexuality. By using the technique of contradiction you will be strengthening your resolve to be free of outside opinion. Maybe you aren't ready to post the letter yet, but simply writing it down helps you clarify the issues in your mind, preparing you for the day when you may have to justify your existence in a face-to-face setting. However gratifying it may be, avoid cheap abuse and try to keep your responses rational.

Sometimes, though, arguments aren't always as straightforward as they seem. What is said appears to be supportive, but then comes an "if" or a "but" which turns the whole thing inside out. Watch out for those pesky ifs or buts. For example, your local vicar might say that he has every respect for gay people and that, like everyone else, they are the children of God. Make sure he isn't attaching some condition like "but they should resist the temptation to indulge in homosexual acts and be penitent for their sins of the flesh".

Or a friend might say he has "nothing against homosexuals" but he thinks they're "more to be pitied than blamed". Is his pity really going to add anything to your dignity?

Apparent sympathisers can be very seductive and, of course, we should welcome supporters wherever we can find them. But don't take anything at face value: examine it, question it and, if necessary, contradict it. It's easy, when we're a little unsure of ourselves, to grab any sign of support, but tread warily. Don't let anybody—whether it's your mother, teacher, doctor or whoever—get away with two-edged sympathy. For the sake of your self-respect (and for their education) don't hesitate to point out the weaknesses in their arguments.

Even if you're isolated at the moment, and still not convinced that you can achieve everything that this book is urging you to, you can still put these techniques of questioning and contradiction into effect. The rethinking of attitudes can begin immediately. If you feel badly about being gay, you need to wash out the distorted, ignorant ideas which have been foisted upon you and listen to your own feelings.

Help yourself by reading some of the excellent material which gays have published for themselves. Read sensible newspapers that will tell you the truth about what is happening inside the gay community. Better still, read the gay press and discover that there is an entirely different angle from which to look at things. You'll see that there is no single "gay lifestyle"—we all make our own. For every one of the millions of homosexuals in the world there is an individual creating a personal interpretation of what it means to be gay.

There is an excitement in releasing yourself from the prison of fear that so many gay people inhabit, but there is also apprehension about what lies outside. Instead of being afraid of this great adventure, embrace it and ensure that you claim your share of the world's supply of happiness. It is waiting out there somewhere.

Tip the balance in your favour and eventually you'll realise that your gayness isn't such a bad thing after all.

2: Coming out

"Coming out" means telling yourself and other people the truth about your sexuality. For those who are emerging from a long period of denial, it can be a terrifying prospect, but coming out is a primary source of liberation.

What holds most of us back is the fear that there will be a terrible reaction. We imagine that our friends, family and colleagues at work will recoil in horror and reject us. After all, haven't we spent our entire lives listening to them deriding "pansies" and despising "nancy boys"? How can we possibly tell these people what we are when they apparently hate us so vehemently? Every day we read in the papers about how terrible we are, how much people condemn us; surely to reveal our true selves would be totally unacceptable?

Or could it be that we are underestimating the ability of our loved ones to change their minds when faced with a real, live, gay person? It's possible that the only images they have are based on the stereotypes which we discussed earlier. Perhaps they haven't thought about the subject in any detail since furtively discussing it over an illicit cigarette in the toilets at school. It is, after all, a common human reaction to be suspicious and afraid of things that we don't understand. Homosexuality is often seen as exotic, and unfamiliar and those gay people who remain silent perpetuate that myth.

Whether they realise it or not, just about everyone knows at least one gay person and everybody has been confronted with the topic at some stage—even if only in newspapers or on television. Gay people are everywhere, and much more visible than they have ever been.

But that doesn't mean that this new prominence has penetrated the centuries-old layers of ignorance. Indeed, when a gay character appears in a soap opera, even when he or she is sympathetically drawn, some viewers will become angry because the topic has been raised at all. The BBC was inundated with complaints when two gay characters in their popular soap opera *Eastenders* gave each other a brief peck on the lips. Despite the media attention that has been given to homosexuality over the past few years, many heterosexuals still find it profoundly shocking and disturbing. The Broadcasting Standards Commission still receives many complaints every time homosexuality is featured on TV.

Whenever gay people choose the option of "passing for straight", it helps the majority to go on imagining that the subject is irrelevant to them and that they can continue with their prejudices undisturbed.

Taking the plunge

It's amazing to see the transformation in attitudes when gay people come out to their straight friends. Instead of the anticipated knee-jerk sniggering reaction, you may well find one of genuine interest and concern. It may start out as curiosity (and there's nothing wrong with that), but it rapidly turns into acceptance.

Take the case of Andrew. He decided to come out to his friend Hannah when they were seventeen:

> I'd known Hannah since we were at school together
> and we'd always been best friends. There was never
> any question of romance or anything like that, we just
> enjoyed each other's company. It had been on my
> mind for quite a while to tell Hannah I was gay,
> although I hadn't told anyone else. I was a bit scared
> in case she fell out with me; she was the only friend I
> had at the time. Anyway, I approached the subject in a
> roundabout sort of way, talking about pop stars who

were bisexual and that sort of thing. Hannah said she thought lesbians were funny and thought one of the teachers at school might be one. Then I just came out with it and said "Hannah, I think I'm queer." She looked at me a bit and then said: "You mean you're gay. You shouldn't call yourself queer." We had a really good talk about it and I told her I felt as though I'd been carrying a sack of coal around on my back and somebody had lifted it off. Then she said: "What are you going to do about it?" and I said I didn't know. She said there was a gay pub in town and why didn't I go there to see what happened. I told her that I was too scared to go on my own, so she went with me.

Andrew was pleasantly surprised that, not only was his best friend totally understanding, she also did something positive to help him.

While making these explorations you might receive a few defensive and predictable responses. People will unthinkingly resort to the clichéd remark or easy joke (like "Backs against the wall lads" and "Don't bend down around here") but these don't necessarily indicate what the response will be to your own coming out. Thinking and speaking in stereotyped ways is common—we all do it. When we are talking about subjects that are apparently unimportant, why bother thinking anything original about them? Much easier to resort to the ready-made joke or the received "wisdom".

Far more important is whether your friend is generally sympathetic, sensible and capable of accepting new ideas.

Not everyone's experience was as easy as Andrew's, though. David was twenty-seven when he came out to his best friend Mike. They had worked together in the same office for five years and become close friends. But David hadn't mentioned his gayness. He felt at the time it wasn't important; he had no gay friends and spent most of his leisure time at home with his parents watching television. He occasionally invented a girlfriend when Mike brought up the subject of sex. Then, one day, quite by accident, David met

Guy and they began an intense gay relationship. David wanted to tell Mike about this exciting new development in his life, but he was afraid of the effect it might have on their friendship:

> I was dropping big hints about "we"—"we" went to the pictures or "we" had a nice meal out, but I suppose he thought it was another of the casual girlfriends I had invented so often. He never asked me who the other half of "we" was. In the end I decided it just had to be done. When I told Mike he went white, as though he simply couldn't believe it. I would never have done it on my own, it was being with Guy that had given me the confidence and determination. Anyway, Mike walked out of the pub looking very angry and slammed the door behind him. I was really upset and didn't sleep for three nights. Mike avoided me at work and, even though I knew he wasn't a gossip, I thought he might tell some of the others in the office, or even the boss. He ignored me for a week and then one day he came up to my desk and said "Are you going to the canteen for lunch?" He told me he'd thought about the whole thing and talked it over with his wife, Maureen, and decided that he'd been a bit unreasonable. He apologised and said would Guy and I like to go over to their house for a meal. It was great, I was so relieved. That was two years ago and the four of us have become close friends. Maureen has been great about it—I think it was she who made Mike see reason—and she has given us lots of good advice.

Although it was an unpleasant experience, David had the good sense to let Mike work it out for himself. Friends who show an initial bad reaction often need a bit of time to get used to this new image of you.

In many cases, friends are already aware of the truth, even though you haven't told them. Some people are more sensitive and perceptive than others and are quite capable of picking up hints. However, it is generally necessary for you to give them "permission" to talk about it. This was what happened to Derek when he decided to tell Gavin and Jean, a couple who ran the local drama group, of which Derek was a member:

> It was after one of the rehearsals, we went to the pub. After a couple of drinks, the subject of gays came up. I think it was because at the time we were doing The Importance of Being Earnest. I said "I suppose you know that Oscar Wilde isn't the only gay person involved with tonight's rehearsal." Jean said, "Thank goodness you've told us, now we can relax!" You could have knocked me down with a feather. When I asked how they knew—because I thought I was really good at covering it up—Jean said, "What do you take us for, idiots?" And that was the end of the conversation. But it was great to be out with them.

Occasionally you will have a reaction that is so bad it causes the friendship to end. This is what happened to Darryl when he told his flatmate:

> Bob and I had been sharing this flat for two years, ever since I'd answered an ad in the local paper. We got on really well, although we'd led completely separate social lives. It was never any trouble living together, we both tried to be sensitive when the other wanted to be on his own. If we both happened to be at home, it was all easy-going and Bob and I had long conversations about all kinds of things. Then one of the conversations came round to sex, and I half-jokingly said I was gay. Well, his face just fell and he started calling me names, the worst names he could think of. I couldn't believe he was talking to me: we'd never had an argument before. I knew he was a bit on the macho side when he was out with his mates, but I'd never been on the receiving end. Anyway, he said

I'd better find somewhere else to live because he didn't want an Aids-carrying queer giving him a disease. He said he was going to throw out all the pots, pans and cutlery and disinfect the whole house. He said I made him sick. At one point I thought he was going to hit me.

It was amazing to see the transformation of a normally reasonable man into a raving bigot. Obviously he had a big hang-up about homosexuality. Perhaps he was insecure about his own feelings or maybe he thought his mates would think there was something strange about him when they found out he was living with a poof. He started locking his bedroom door as though I was going to rape him or something. After a week I couldn't stand it any more, and although it was very inconvenient, I started looking round for somewhere else to live. When I told Bob he just said "Good" and went into his room. I moved out three weeks later and he didn't even say cheerio.

If you get a reaction like this then you have to recognise that the person has a problem. It has been termed "homophobia"— an irrational fear of homosexuals. The recent willingness of society to examine the topic of homosexuality has brought an inevitable reaction, and homophobia is very much to the fore in some quarters. People who were previously indifferent are now angry and frightened by the knowledge that homosexuals are not the irrelevant minority they had imagined. Misunderstandings and ignorance about Aids can also cause irrational reactions.

But there is no need for you to feel guilty when other people can't cope with their own feelings. What kind of friend is it, anyway, who would want to keep you in an emotional prison just so he or she won't feel uncomfortable? Maybe the kind of friend you'd be better off without.

To summarise:
- Drop a few hints first of all to "test the water". Sometimes hints are all that are needed to get the ball rolling.
- Make sure you are emotionally prepared for a bad reaction. It probably won't come, but if it does, don't let it diminish your resolve.
- Be ready to talk to your friends for hours about the subject. They'll probably be very curious and want to know what it's about and what it means for your friendship. Make sure you're well-informed yourself in order to do all this successfully.
- You might lose a friend. In some people the revulsion to homosexuality is so deep-rooted they simply cannot overcome it. It's their problem, not yours.
- If there is an unspoken understanding between you and your friends, it might be that they are waiting for you to give them permission to talk openly about the subject.

Coming out at work

Those of us who have jobs spend half our waking lives at work. Clearly, it would make life much easier and more pleasant if we could come out in the working environment. For some gays this presents no problem, but for others it is a risky business, carrying with it the distinct possibility of becoming unemployed.

This is one area of coming out where I would counsel caution. You are the only one who can honestly assess your situation, especially the likely reactions of your colleagues and the attitudes of the boss. If it becomes known in a workplace that a person is gay, the gossip, baiting and teasing, especially of young people, can be extremely cruel. Whether you work in an office or factory, a school or some other institution, you have to ask yourself if you could cope with the potential isolation or taunting when unsympathetic workmates get to know.

Tony worked as a male nurse in a large general hospital. He made no secret of his gayness among his colleagues and was generally well liked and accepted. However, also working in the hospital was a porter who would make a point of cat-calling insults whenever he saw Tony in the corridor:

> Whenever this man saw me he would call out things like "Here comes the Middlesex Regiment" and "What time is it, nancy boy?" He always ensured that he did it in front of an audience. It made me feel uncomfortable and humiliated at first, but after a while I began to think "If I'm genuinely not ashamed of being gay, how can I be insulted if someone says I am?" I thought about something I'd read by Eleanor Roosevelt which always stuck in my mind: "Nobody can make you feel inferior without your consent." So I decided I wasn't going to give my consent and started letting the insults roll off my back and eventually managed to ignore them totally. I just behaved as though this horrible man wasn't there. Without a reaction he soon tired of it. He realised that not everyone thought it was funny and were questioning his motives for doing it.

Occasionally this kind of incident can work in your favour by actually pushing straight colleagues into giving you their support. But, for you, ignoring the taunts is by far the best way of dealing with them. Develop a technique of non-reaction. However hard it may be, pretending indifference is definitely the most effective method. Arguing or shouting back tends to be counterproductive, unless you have a devastating wit or a louder voice than anybody else. If your tormentor can "get you going" he has achieved his end. Answering back always means a lot of wasted energy which is needed for more important and constructive battles.

Physical retaliation is sometimes a temptation. Resist it. Punch-ups are not only undignified, they are also dangerous. If you are threatened with violence (and regrettably it does sometimes happen) you might like to consider pursuing the matter with your boss or union. There is now also a legal redress that might be useful in situations like this. Under the

Criminal Justice Act of 1994 a new crime of "intentional harassment" was created. Originally intended to deal with racial harassment, the offence now covers all types of intentional harassment. The Government said during debate on the Bill that the clause would cover disabled people and homosexuals, so it might be a useful weapon not only in connection with employment but also other kinds of harassment. Seek legal advice if you want to explore this.

If none of this works, then you might ask whether you want to stay in the job. If your employer has an equal opportunities policy which includes protecting the rights of gay people, you might want to bring a complaint under its provisions. The thought of losing their jobs might make your tormentors feel less inclined to bully you.

Some gay people in supervisory positions fear that their authority will be undermined if they come out. Once again, it is something only you can accurately gauge, but if you honestly believe that such a revelation would cause your staff to lose respect for you, then perhaps their respect isn't as secure as you imagine anyway. There are gays in senior positions who have found their sexuality has proved no bar to their career progress, even though their colleagues were aware of their orientation. Dignity and a sense of humour are potent weapons in this situation, as well as being good at your job.

An article in the American business magazine *Fortune* (16 December 1991) looked at the effects of coming out on executives in some of the USA's largest corporations. "Most gay and lesbian executives who have done it find the fear of coming out is worse than the reality." The article quotes one gay executive as saying that he believes the answer to gay-bashing is more openness. "Familiarity breeds respect, not contempt," he says, "I look for funny or unthreatening ways to remind people I'm gay."

Another American, James Woods, has studied the coping strategies of 100 gay men in corporate life ranging in age from twenty-one to sixty-eight and in rank from a man four months out of college to the Chief Executive Officer of a large pharmaceutical company. Woods identified three groups: 'counterfeiters', who invent a heterosexual identity for themselves (sometimes even marrying); 'integrators', who are known to be gay; and the biggest group, 'avoiders'. Avoiders are the people who say things like "I don't deny it, but then again, I don't confirm it." They just hope the issue will never arise at their workplace. The article says: "They don't join the gang for drinks after work. Ask how their weekend went, and they'll answer, 'Okay, didn't do much.' If you stop to think about it—which avoiders pray you won't—you realise that you know nothing about them."

Forward-looking companies are now offering their gay employees some kind of recognition. This is particularly true in America, where the gay community is much better organised than in Britain, and presses for rights to be recognised. Eventually these new policies will find their way into British companies, and this will help homosexuals feel free to pursue their careers and their personal lives without one destroying the other. However, unless companies know they have gay employees in need of special consideration (in regard to their pension arrangements, compassionate leave etc.), then they will not see the need to make changes. In this respect, we all have a duty to each other and ourselves to be as open as we can.

For those in a "position of trust" (which usually means the care of children or the mentally incapable) there is a great deal of prejudice to be countered. It is unfairly assumed that gay people cannot be trusted with children, when in fact they are often very good with them. Gay people are often drawn to teaching and allied professions because they can find a sort of surrogate family in such work. Coming out in a job which involves young children can be risky. Many have done it and succeeded, while others have been involved in prolonged and bitter battles, which are frequently lost. Campaigns are afoot to have the working rights of homosexuals recognised.

Campaigners are attempting to reduce—and even totally outlaw—discrimination against homosexuals at work, including in pensions.

Prejudice and discrimination at work caused by fear of Aids has at last diminished to the point where it is now rarely an issue. Relentless education campaigns by the unions and by gay people have ensured that the ignorance that prompted these reactions has now been virtually eliminated. If there is any element of Aids hysteria in your work-place, it is very important that it is challenged. Get expert advice, help and support. Some unions—particularly the public service ones— have taken the matter very seriously and have worked hard to introduce sensible and humane policies to protect their members from discrimination. Check with your representative. Then try to arrange for one of the Aids support groups to come and calm the fears of your colleagues. Your local switchboard or one of the specialist Aids organisations can help.

Just a few thoughts in conclusion:

- Coming out is a seminal experience for gay people and an essential step in the struggle for happiness.

- Sometimes reactions will be bad, but most of the time they won't be. You are the best judge of who you want to tell and what the consequences of unexpected homophobia might be. Don't let the fear of disapproval deter you— what kind of a friend is that wants to keep you imprisoned in the closet?

- Take care when coming out at work. Ask yourself these questions before doing it: Is there any evidence that my colleagues are homophobic? Is there any evidence that the boss is anti-gay? Does the firm/organisation I work for have an equal opportunities policy? Does my union have a commitment to protecting its gay members from discrimination? Are any of my colleagues already 'out'— if so what has been their experience? Do my colleagues like me enough to take the news with equanimity? Can I safely share the truth about my sexuality with selected colleagues?

- Having made the sometimes enormous effort to come out to friends and work colleagues, many gays have reported a new era of happiness and relaxation in their lives.

3. Coming out at home

If you have no family or have broken off relations with them, then this chapter may not be relevant. But if, like most people, you still have strong ties with your family, being honest about your sexuality could improve your relationship with them considerably.

There can be little doubt that most parents exercise an inordinately strong influence on their children. From the day we are born they have authority over us, they are our guardians and strongly influence our decisions. With luck they will love and protect us until we are capable of fending for ourselves. The difficulty often comes in recognising when the time has arrived for children to strike out on their own. Parents may be reluctant to let go because they have come to see their children as the mainspring of their own fulfilment.

Merely moving out of the family home does not necessarily mean the achievement of complete independence from parents. Some parental influences continue until late in life, even when great distances separate family members. It's not unusual to see middle-aged men and women still slightly afraid of their parents, still manipulated and made to feel guilty, even after they have established their own lives and families. Thus, even though this chapter will apply mainly to younger people, it will also have relevance for many older gay men.

Living at your parents' home

Because most "out" gay people do not marry, there is usually less urgency for them to leave their parents' home. While living under the same roof, gay people are likely to find it hard to resist parental pressure. Younger people may also be financially dependent on their parents.

For most gay people living in the parental home, mum and dad are the last people they'd consider talking to about their sexuality. There are exceptions to this, of course.

Parents, in turn, have high expectations of their off-spring. The assumption will be that they are heterosexual and Mum and Dad will regard marriage and production of grandchildren as a foregone conclusion. The gay son or daughter will almost certainly be unwilling or unable to carry through these expectations. Parents, particularly those with no heterosexual children, often resent being "denied" grandchildren, and this leads to feelings of guilt and fear for the son or daughter. The son or daughter will worry that parents, who seem secure and certain in their sexuality, will never understand anything that differs from it.

In a state of isolation, the fear of not being able to "deliver the goods" grows ever more dismaying. Most gay people have, at some point in their lives, gone to great lengths to hide their gayness from their parents. The mere prospect of them finding out causes jelly legs and cold sweats. It is obvious that these intense fears are a giant barrier to attaining happiness. There is only one way to change this state of affairs and that is to be completely honest with your parents.

This means you!

Many readers will be snorting with derision at the very idea of coming out to parents. A million reasons why they couldn't contemplate such a thing spring to their lips. The prospect seems outrageous. However, it is an unavoidable fact that you will not be happy as a homosexual until you stop regarding your loved ones as a source of fear and apprehension.

I recently gave a talk to a gay youth group in London, and we raised the topic of coming out at home. I asked how many had told their parents, and out of the fifty or so people who were present, only a tiny handful had taken the step. The others all had, as far as they were concerned, perfectly good reasons why they couldn't do it. These mostly revolved around the idea that parents were old and couldn't cope with the news ("Why upset them at this time in their lives?"). Some even thought that the revelation would cause one or both parents to drop immediately to the ground with a cardiac arrest. Others were worried that their parents were "right-wing" (one even described his father as "an old fascist") and couldn't possibly understand. They had expressed racist and homophobic opinions in the past, and therefore would not be able to understand if they had a gay child.

How many of these reasons are valid, and how many are just excuses?

Naturally, if your parents genuinely do have a heart condition, and are under doctor's orders not to be stressed or upset, then you might have to consider your position carefully. But chronic ill-health should not be used as a cop-out. And if parents really are reactionary in their opinions, and have indicated that they do not like homosexuals—well, now is the time to consider challenging those opinions.

The Observer newspaper commissioned an opinion poll which asked parents what they would do if they discovered that their teenage child was having a homosexual relationship: 59% said they would "try to put a stop to it" and 27% said they would "advise against it"; another 10% said they "wouldn't interfere" and 4% "didn't know". I think it was the final 4% who were being most honest in this instance. What people say cold to an opinion pollster and what they say when faced with the situation in their own home with their own flesh and blood are not necessarily the same. And, indeed, another poll, conducted by the London Gay Teenage Group among gays who had actually taken the step and come out at home, told a different story:

Some 28% said they had received a "good" reaction from their parents when they revealed their homosexuality. Another 18% said they had received a "reasonable" reaction and 8.6% said they had met with "indifference". A further 8.6% of parents had thought it was "a phase" while 17% reported a "bad" reaction and 10% said it was "terrible". And finally 10% said they had got a "mixed" reaction—one parent's good, the other's bad.

But you shouldn't be put off by these figures. I'm convinced that if a follow-up poll were to be conducted with the same people, it would be found that most of them, if not all, had eventually sorted out their differences with their parents—at least to the point of tolerance.

Everybody's experience is different. Some of the young people in the survey had "dropped a bomb" without thinking through their approach and were totally unprepared for the tornado of emotion which followed their announcement. You can learn a lot from these pioneers and be prepared for most eventualities.

It is at this point that we have to face a hard truth. There is a distinct possibility that things will get worse before they get better. The inescapable fact is that you are going to have to face the consequences of your actions. If you don't take the step and continue to find spurious reasons for not taking it, then you are going to waste much valuable time in your drive for a happier life.

But, you might say, how could I possibly be happy if I go and cause my old mum and dad such misery? Life won't be worth living; I'll be intensely miserable, there'll be a terrible atmosphere in the house and everybody will be anything but happy. This may well be true, but it will be a temporary upset, a sharp pain which will eventually fade. The consequences of not doing it are a lifetime of niggling doubts and gut-churning fears:

"Do they know that the letter I got today was from *Gay Times*?"

"Will they ask where I've been when I get back from the gay pub?"

"Will someone ring up when I'm not at home and accidentally give the game away?"

Consider this, written by May Sarton, a lesbian writer: "Sometimes I wonder whether what is often wrong with intimate human relations is not recognising the necessity for suffering. We fear disturbance, change, fear to bring to light and talk about what is painful. Suffering often feels like failure, but it is actually the door to growth. And growth does not cease to be painful at any age."

The unspoken knowledge excuse

An excuse often tendered for not doing anything about the home situation is: "Well, I'm sure they know, but they don't want to talk about it. It's sort of understood." This excuse gives rise to a false sense of security which just puts off the day when you can be at ease with your sexuality, and honest with those around you.

The "unspoken knowledge" idea might well have some truth in it. Parents generally aren't fools and many of them know about their child's "difference", albeit on a subconscious level. They might imagine that if they don't confront the knowledge, keep it tucked away in the back of their mind, unnamed, the pain need never be faced. After all, if it remains unspoken, it might just turn out not to be true. But while this goes on it means the maintenance of a debilitating pretence for the gay person which drains the spirit. Both sides in this tacit agreement are losers, but it is the gay person who loses the most.

Now is the time to face the inevitable and to start considering not if, but how and when you are going to tackle the problem. True, it will be difficult and uncomfortable, but the period of turmoil will eventually dwindle and, unless you are very unlucky, your parents will come to accept you for what you are. They may not like it at first, there may be some resistance, but if you persist and are dignified about the whole thing, then progress will be made. This has been the experience of most gay people who have already taken the plunge. They have emerged from living in constant fear into a happier and more relaxed time when the burden of possible discovery has been lifted from them. This is how one gay man, Jon, told the story:

> I had spent the three years since I was fifteen frightened to death of the feelings I was having. I knew I was different from my friends but I didn't know what to do about it. I had a good relationship with my parents on most things, but we'd never talked much about sex or our private feelings. When I discovered I was attracted to other men, and the attraction was very strong, I decided to tell my mother. I didn't know how she'd react because we'd never talked about anything like this before. I was terrified, but decided it had to be done. I just sort of blurted it out on Sunday morning when she was peeling some potatoes. She was shocked at first, and had to sit down, but she didn't scream and shout as I thought she might. She thought about it for a moment and then said, if that's how it was, we'd just have to get on with it. We had a good long chat about things in general, and about where I could get help—not to be cured of being gay, but to find other people who I could talk to. She was very worried about Aids, but I managed to calm her down over that one and assured her that I hadn't done anything that would lay me open to catching it. I said I had found out as much as I could about it, and I intended to be very cautious and sensible. I have a feeling that she might have had her suspicions for a long time, so this was really only confirmation.

Many people have shared Jon's experience; they were pleasantly surprised by the supportive response they got from their parents. They have the very comforting knowledge that whatever else might happen in life, their parents' love and concern will remain with them.

Of course, things might not go so smoothly for everyone, and even parents who say that they are accepting and supportive might, underneath, be churning with anger or guilt or self-blame. They need time to make the adjustment. Don't expect too much from them straight away—after all, this might have been a complete shock to them. They have to have time to reconstruct their ideas about who you are. They had imagined that you were a heterosexual person, who would follow the heterosexual pattern of marriage and children. For them suddenly to discover that you aren't this person is a trauma for some parents, and it might take them a number of years before they can get their mind to accept this new version of you. They may have a lot of thinking to do and many prejudices to overcome. The better informed you are, the more likely you are to be able to help them with any questions they might have. You cannot rush this process, and so don't be impatient if your parents fail to react with joy and celebration when you tell them you are gay. They might well think, initially, that it is the end of the world. You have to respect that any feelings of failure, guilt and self-blame are real for them, however unreasonable they may seem to you. All you can do is to continue to reassure them. Demonstrate that you are not a walking tragedy, and that you will continue to function as a well-adjusted human being—even though you've turned out to be "one of them".

Like everyone else, parents have been raised to be suspicious, if not downright hostile, to homosexuality. You can't expect them to shrug off a lifetime's indoctrination overnight. The good news is that although prejudices are notoriously difficult to overcome, there is a way that they can be beaten. Research has shown that prejudice is not controlled by the rational and logical part of our mind, but by its emotional responses. Therefore, it is very difficult for people to be "educated" or "persuaded" out of a strongly-held prejudice without a personal, emotional experience that challenges the very core of that prejudice. Your coming out may provide that personal, emotional experience. Salvaging their relationship with their child is a pretty strong motivation to challenge their fears and ignorance. To do this, they also need facts—make sure you have them to hand. A few preparations can be helpful:

- Ring a gay helpline and tell them what you intend to do. It's a great morale booster to talk it over with someone who has already succeeded.
- Give your parents supportive and well-informed books to read. Try my book for parents-and-families-of-gays *A Stranger in the Family: How to cope if your child is gay* (The Other Way Press).
- Give parents the contact numbers and addresses of parents-of-gays helplines (listed at the back of this book) so they can talk it over with others who have already been through this crisis and survived. Really encourage parents to do this, it is probably the most constructive and helpful step they can take in their struggle for acceptance.
- Try to enlist the support of someone else within the family. If you have brothers and sisters, tell them first so that when you come to tell your parents, your siblings can give them a lead. Often parents don't know how to react, they don't know what they think, and they don't know what to do. Brothers and sisters who are casually accepting, and don't consider it any big deal can have an amazing, calming effect on parents. The success of this tactic depends, of course, on the relationship you have with your brothers and sisters—if they're much younger than you, or they're likely to be hostile, then this might not be the right course of action. If there is no-one in the family who is suitable, see if you can find a family friend or someone else who is willing to support you.

Breaking the news

Choose a time when you won't be disturbed and when you'll have your parents' undivided attention. Take the plunge, but gently. Try not to make it sound like the announcement of some great tragedy. It's momentous, but not disastrous. Be gentle about it, but at the same time don't give the impression that you aren't determined or confident about what you are doing. For a change you're probably going to have to teach them something. Positive information about homosexuality is thin on the ground in the straight world and it's unlikely that they'll have given the matter deep thought. The information that they will have taken in from newspapers and television documentaries will have left them with the impression that homosexuals are either totally corrupt or inevitably doomed to a lingering death. Be ready to lighten their darkness.

There is a possibility that they will refuse to accept what you say. They may try to dismiss it as a phase or some kind of attention-seeking ploy on your part. If this happens, you might feel an overwhelming urge to take the escape route it offers and let the matter drop. Who needs this kind of shattering confrontation anyway? But you can't let it drop if you've got this far. However much your parents may insist that it is a non-issue because it's all "self-delusion" or "a misunderstanding", or "a phase" they cannot really ignore what they've just heard. They will *know* even if they purport to disbelieve you. This is what happened to Darren:

> When I told them, Mum said: "Don't be so silly, you're just confused. As you get a little older you'll come to realise that this is just a phase you're going through and you'll start to fancy girls. All boys go through this." I tried to insist that it wasn't a phase and that I'd felt like this ever since I could remember, but she wouldn't discuss it. She kept saying that it was something I would grow out of and not to worry. Dad didn't say anything, he just sort of retired behind his newspaper. I don't know whether he was embarrassed or what. But there was no way that I could get beyond my mother's insistence that I was mixed up about homosexuality, and that I didn't really understand what it meant. In the end, I just said: "Look, mum, I know why you don't want to believe it, but it's true.

You may wish it weren't, but I'm afraid I've got my
life to live. And I'm going to live it. I hope that you'll
talk to me about it when you're ready."

Darren was confident enough to be able to see what his
mother was doing. He recognised that she was using denial as
a defence mechanism against news that she simply didn't
want to hear. Many other parents don't claim it to be a phase,
but they do refuse to discuss it. They imagine that if they
push it away it will disappear. It is too painful for them to
deal with and so they cope by refusing to acknowledge it. If
you get an "I don't want to talk about it" response from your
parents, you have to leave them for a while to let the news
penetrate their defences. You will have to raise the topic
again, maybe at frequent intervals, until they let the news in
and begin to deal with it. At that point you may get a
dramatic—even melodramatic—reaction. You have to let
your parents have this outpouring of feeling, even though it
may result in them saying hurtful and untrue things about
you. Let them get it out of their system, and try not to be too
devastated by any signs of initial rejection or revulsion which
they might display. Acknowledge that receiving the news
might bring on a violent reaction, and prepare yourself for it.

Once again, time is the great ally here. Give your parents
time to deal with their initial feelings. Make sure they have
support, in the shape of the books and telephone numbers we
talked about earlier, and then leave it for a while. Maybe they
will want to talk immediately, maybe you will have to wait
until they're ready. Once again, please try to understand that
this can be a shattering experience for some parents, and only
time, understanding, love and positive information will allow
them to recover.

Where did we go wrong?

There may be emotional pressures from parents that are hard
to counter. Self-blame is a common one; they will almost
invariably ask: "Where did we go wrong?" You can assure

them that they have done nothing wrong, and that there is no convincing evidence to support the dominant mother/weak father theory of homosexuality. You should let them know that you consider yourself to be well-adjusted and rational, and that when the excitement has died down, things will be much as they were before. Whatever they might think at that moment, it isn't really the catastrophe they imagine. Assure them that you are happy, and that they can be, too, if they choose to be.

Another possible reaction is anger. Feelings about homosexuality go very deep for some people: it is still one of the major taboos of our society, and despite the fact that it has had such a high profile over the past few years, there is still a great deal of misunderstanding surrounding it. Rage is the first reaction of a minority of people when the subject is even mentioned. When asked to explain this extreme anger, such individuals are often unable to say why they are so agitated. They will thrash around for a rationale, but will be unable to come up with one that stands examination.

Your parents, if they suffer from this reaction, might threaten to throw you out, tell you they are ashamed of you, write you out of their wills, or try to force you to have psychiatric treatment. Even in the face of such forceful anger, let them see that you are strong enough to be what you are without apology. This is new territory for them, and they're probably extremely confused. They will need a lead. You can give it to them by not letting their initial negative reactions gain any credence in the conversation. Repeat and repeat—as many times as necessary—that you are secure, happy and unashamed. Counter any arguments they may throw at you with reason and logic. Don't be drawn into a slanging match, however tempting it might be. If you're angry about the things they are saying, then acknowledge that anger, tell them that they are hurting your feelings, but don't try to hurt them back.

Some young people relate to their parents on a more forceful, challenging level, but if you want to succeed in your coming out, resist the temptation to bring into the conversation all kinds of other issues that are unconnected. Leave all that for another time.

Don't expect the whole matter to be over in five minutes. Your parents might misunderstand your motives for coming out, they may imagine that it is some roundabout way of hurting them because they feel they have failed you as parents. Their thoughts might turn to what future life might be like for you as a gay person, and this may dismay them, too. Remember, they have read all the horror stories in the newspapers, and seen the often tragic and ridiculous portrayals of gays on television. They will be aware of Aids. These are major issues for them to face up to and think about, and they won't be resolved quickly.

It's very upsetting to see beloved parents in pain, but they have to be made aware that any attempt to force you back into the closet will only result in more friction. The shock might be quite profound, but with the right kind of help and a bit of effort on their part, they will recover. The grief they experience will ultimately benefit them. After all, life is full of unwanted turnabouts: this is one with a constructive end product.

Most parents adjust eventually to the news that their child is gay. Some are completely accepting, some retain reservations, many have suspected the truth for some time and are relieved that it is out in the open.

Those who counsel parents-of-gays say that often at the beginning mums and dads experience a sort of pseudo-bereavement. They feel they have lost the child they knew and he or she has been replaced by this other person who seems like a stranger.

So, a period of "mourning" for what they imagined was the "old you" must be allowed. During that period many parents have found that they have also gained something valuable which they didn't have before: a truly honest and open adult relationship with their son or daughter. An invisible curtain of tension is lifted, and a new era of communication begins.

During this period of adjustment (and you really do have to let them make it in their own time) you must be careful not to be dragged into the depression which might temporarily settle. Your parents are thinking the issue through, trying to make sense of it in their own minds. They may need to talk to someone outside. Try to ensure that whoever they choose to share their feelings with—whether it's a family friend, doctor or teacher—knows what they are talking about and is not simply going to reinforce or inflame existing prejudices or fears.

Ensure also that you have all the available facts about Aids. Even if your parents are prepared to accept your orientation, they may have deep misgivings about its association with Aids. Their love for you naturally leads to concern about your health and safety. Once more, give them sensible literature to read—there is plenty available. Reassure them that you know the dangers and that you are going to be sensible and careful.

When they are ready to talk to you further, try to be candid. In some instances parents may not wish to seek outside counselling. They feel it is something to be kept within the family, and they will look to you for the facts. I realise that this won't be possible in families where talking intimately is not part of the ethos. In these cases, perhaps it is better to let parents think the issues through for themselves, making the helpful literature available to them when it's required, and remaining dignified and determined throughout.

Coming out from afar

If you already live away from home, but still have strong family connections, you should think about seeing your parents for the sole purpose of telling them, or if that isn't possible, writing them a letter. Perhaps you are already living in a relationship which they know about and think of as "platonic" or "just good friends". It could be that they suspect its true nature, but as long as it doesn't have a name they don't have to think about it. This is not satisfactory. It means that you will constantly have to make excuses, pretend and lie. It will inevitably have a detrimental effect on the gay relationship, too. So give it a name. Tell them that you have a special friend or a lover or a partner or whatever other term you use to describe him. They might not like it, but then again they may be relieved and happy that you aren't alone. What many parents fear most for their child is not so much homosexuality as a life of rejection and isolation.

Parents have been known to accept a son's or daughter's same-sex partner enthusiastically. Many gay people report that their families have come to regard their lovers as valuable and much-loved additions to the tribe. One research project in America suggested that if gay people simply present their partner to the family without explanation, it can take an average of five years before the necessary trust and familiarity has built up and the partner can be fully accepted and integrated into the family. But if you are up front and honest from the beginning, families can much sooner give you the support and acceptance that your relationship needs. It also dignifies your relationship, and makes everyone aware that you take it seriously.

The third party syndrome

Parents may discover the truth from a concerned (or occasionally vindictive) third party. Or they may have come across intimate diaries and letters or have overheard their children's telephone calls.

If you are "dragged out" rather than coming out voluntarily, you should still try to salvage the situation. When parents confront you, it is likely that you will be taken off-guard. It is tempting in your panic to deny everything, but this just makes matters worse. Far better to approach it from the "it's a fair cop" point of view and conduct yourself with as much dignity as you can muster.

The big problem, when parents find out from a third party, is that they are more likely to approach the revelation from a negative angle. The issue will be clouded in an atmosphere of your being caught red-handed, and it will be just that bit more difficult to explain why you were keeping it from them if you truly don't think it's shameful. If you find yourself in the third party situation, turn the tables as soon as possible and start on the reassurance. It is likely that your parents have spent some time imagining the worst and getting themselves worked into a frenzy of guilt and recrimination. Let them know straight away that you don't accept their definition of your sexuality as undesirable or inferior. As soon as you can, give them something positive to read and suggest a counselling service.

Don't tell anyone else

Some parents have pleaded and cajoled their gay son or daughter not to let brothers and sisters, aunts and uncles or grandparents into the "terrible secret". This, too, must be resisted. If you are going to be a happy homosexual, you will have to reach the stage where you can honestly say that you don't care who knows. But you won't get there by being selective with your family. "Don't tell Grandma, you know how fond she is of you," Mum might say. It might seem callous to encourage you to upset an old lady, but if she's that fond of you, she'll cope. Research has shown that elderly people take the news much better than middle-aged people do. It's thought that their experience, and their desire to keep the family together, make them more understanding and much less shockable than their own children.

Yes, you are putting a lot on the line. In a way you are putting the family's love to the test. You are asking them to confirm that they really love you. But you aren't doing it just to upset them: there is an important conclusion to all this— your happiness. And, in the end, granting you this freedom won't cost them a thing. In effect, you are saying: "If you really love me, you'll accept me for what I am and not for what you want me to be." For some people, this is the very definition of love.

We've explored some of the possible consequences of your decision to come out. But there are a few other considerations which we have to take into account. First of all, research has shown that those who are most likely to have big problems when they find out they have a gay child are those people with strong religious convictions, and those who have a very conforming or authoritarian personality.

We have seen that religions often have a very hostile approach to homosexuality. Those people who take their religion seriously may well be thrown into turmoil when they discover that one of their own children is gay. They feel that if they completely accept their child's sexuality, then they will be compromising the religious feelings which are so important to them. Some Christians, however, are quite positive about gay people. You can get some excellent books on this topic from the Lesbian and Gay Christian Movement (address at the back of this book) or from gay book shops. Make sure your parents have these books at their disposal if they are finding problems reconciling their faith with your homosexuality. Others have made the transition from dogma-bound fundamentalism to liberal Christianity, and your parents may be able to make that leap, too. If they can't, and often they can't, then you have to make the decision about what is most important to you. You can continue to develop your own life on the lines that your conscience and heart demand, and hope that your parents will one day accept. Or you may feel that separating yourself from them might be a better answer, relieving you of their demoralising criticism and disapproval. Maybe one day they will think again, when they see that perhaps the biblical condemnations of homosexuality do not seem appropriate to those homosexuals who live decent, honest and fruitful lives.

Those parents who have a strictly conforming approach to life can also be a problem. Often such people were raised in families where rules were obeyed and authority never questioned. They feel strongly that life has a fixed pattern and that there must be no deviation from it. For such people, homosexuality is beyond the pale. They may subscribe to all the familiar stereotypes about homosexuals and also have many negative ideas ("Homosexuals are all promiscuous, they devalue sex, it isn't natural, they aren't normal, they're anything but gay" etc. etc.). When they discover that one of their own children is gay they are thrown into utter confusion and may feel that their whole way of life has been threatened. They may fear the reaction of the neighbours and their work colleagues when it comes out that they have raised a homosexual. They will worry that their highly-valued esteem in the community will be damaged.

How do you cope with such parents, their irrationality and their unyielding concepts of right and wrong?

The only answer is patience, persistence and the maintenance of dignity. You need to be as strong as they are in your conviction that you are right. But you also have to give them time to make the adjustments. It may take longer than it does for most people. Everything we've said so far applies to them, but you must be absolutely confident about yourself, your sexuality and what you want from them before you tell them.

Ethnic communities

Ethnic minorities will have an extra burden. Not only will homosexuality probably be even more severely proscribed than it is in the majority culture, there is also the problem of racism to face.

Young people from Asian or West Indian origins who discover that they are gay may feel extremely wary about telling their family about this. In so many minority communities the family has a dominating role, and all members are expected to be married and produce children. The pressure to do so is intense. Telling your family that you are gay can cause a huge conflict to arise because you will be seen to be breaking what is regarded as an unbreakable tradition. You will be committing the ultimate sin of letting down the family.

However Westernised young people from minority communities might be, they still need their family to provide a bulwark against the racism which is endemic in our society. They are faced with racism and homophobia from the majority culture and homophobia from within their own culture. If they decide to be honest about their sexuality, they may find themselves excluded from the community which can provide so much support against hostility from the majority culture.

Being cast out like this is a serious disadvantage for anyone from an ethnic minority. Your family may be oppressive about your gayness, but it will be that much more difficult for you to function in the world outside without their support. You may become disconnected from your roots.

Fortunately, there are Asian and black groups for gay people, which can provide the kind of support and comradeship that might help you deal with this particularly difficult situation. Call them, go to their meetings, meet others who are in the same situation and see how they have coped.

The worst-case scenario

What happens if it all goes badly wrong and your parents decide they simple can't accept and ask you to leave?

I'm afraid I don't have an answer for this. Each person must make his or her own decision, and that means also accepting the consequences. If you find that your parents reject you completely after you've told them the truth, then the time has come for you to move into the world on your own. It might be difficult, but it won't be impossible. This problem has been recognised, and there are agencies, such as The Albert Kennedy Trust, that can help young people with the immediate problems of homelessness. Get in touch with one of the support organisations or Lesbian and Gay Switchboard and ask for a contact number. Some local authorities, too, will give priority to young gay people who have been thrown out of their home. Check them out.

The longer term emotional problems will be harder, and distressing to resolve. Your own mighty battle has the ultimate aim of freeing you from other people's manipulations, to find your place in the world as a whole human being with a right to pursue the life of your own choosing.

When you prove to your parents that their fears are unfounded and that you can survive your great upheaval, they will probably think again. This was certainly the case with Rob, who came out to his parents when he was sixteen:

> I told my parents that I was gay after I'd met a man who was ten years older than myself. They went through the roof. They told me I was no son of theirs and that they didn't want me in the house. My dad actually threw some of my stuff out of the bedroom window into the street. I thought I was going to go and live with my friend, but when he found out what had happened he got cold feet and said it was all over. He was scared that my parents were going to report him to the police.
>
> So, with nowhere to go, I decided to go to London because I'd heard there was a big gay community there and I might be able to get myself sorted out. But it wasn't as easy as that. I ended up sleeping rough for a few nights before this man came up to me and gave me a card for a counselling organisation for young, homeless people. They managed to get me into a hostel until I could move into a place of my own.
>
> I wouldn't recommend this course of action to anyone else, it was one of the worst times in my life, and I was lucky that it wasn't a whole lot worse. But as it turned out, my parents had done me a favour. I hadn't called them after what they did, but I found out from a man who worked for a missing person agency that they were looking for me.
>
> After three years without contacting them I gave them a ring. My mother was in tears saying how sorry she was and how differently they thought about it now. Strangely, the boot was on the other foot and they were asking me to understand. I'm afraid I will take a long time to forgive them, but in a way I'm relieved to

know that they don't still hate me. I'm not ready to go back and try to make them understand what I've been through because of them and their attitudes.

I'm not ready to say that what they did was OK, because it wasn't. It could have destroyed my life completely. It was sheer luck that I dropped on my feet. I know there are a lot of other people out there on the streets—and in the graveyards—who didn't manage so well.

I've made an independent life and I now no longer need to live in fear of my family. I suppose the day may come when I want to build bridges, but it isn't yet.

4. Finding gay friends

"I think the primary distinction between homosexuals and heterosexuals in our society is not that they are attracted to different genders, and certainly not that their sexual lives and needs are radically different from each other. It is that homosexuals, by default as much as anything else, have managed to sustain a society of friendship that is, for the most part, unequalled by almost any other part of society." - Andrew Sullivan

For the gay man who is just coming to terms with his sexuality, one of the most urgent priorities is finding other gay people. This is important for several reasons, not the least of which is the reassurance and confidence which grows from seeing others who have successfully managed to integrate their homosexuality into their overall lifestyle. There is also the question of finding friends with common experiences who really know what they're talking about. And, of course, that elusive lover who will help us give expression to the need to love and be loved (and can also help us get our rocks off, which is an urgent priority for most young gay men).

Gay friends can support each other in unique ways. Often, groups of friends become a sort of family to each other. The closeness that develops in these sorts of situations can be an excellent antidote to the isolation which otherwise might have to be faced. Many surveys have shown that gay people place great importance on their friendships, and many endure throughout their lives.

But how do gays find each other in the first place? I'm glad to say it's never been easier. Since the law was changed in 1967 the situation has improved immeasurably. Before then, one of the few ways of meeting other homosexual men (except by pure accident) was in a public lavatory. "Cottaging"—as searching for partners in public loos is called—is still a widely used as a form of contact. It is, needless to say, frighteningly dangerous. The lavatories frequented by men looking for sex are well known to the police. Occasionally these places are kept under close surveillance and the men who go there will be systematically arrested. These arrests can run into dozens a day from a single lavatory.

A study carried out in America found that a large proportion of men who seek sex in this way are, in fact, married with children and don't think of themselves as gay. These are the people who most fear public exposure and are, ironically, the ones most likely to end up being charged with a sexual offence. In such cases suicides are not unknown and the attendant disgrace has ruined many a worthy citizen.

There is another danger: cottages are known not only by the police but also by thugs intent on an occasional spot of "queer-bashing". In the past few years there have been several well-publicised cases of gay men being severely beaten, and even murdered, in these circumstances.

Malcolm is a forty-seven year old council workman and no-one knows better than he the terror of being confronted by a gang of youths who regarded him as "just a poofter" and therefore fair game:

> I started cottaging when I was seventeen. It's all there was in those days, and I've been doing it on and off for twenty years now. I never talked to the people I had sex with; it was just a matter of getting it over as quickly as possible and getting out. Then late one night I was using the cottage in the park when I was followed in by a gang of yobs. They called me a few names and then beat me up and stole my wallet watch.

I had two broken ribs and a tooth knocked out. I went to the hospital for treatment, and when they asked what had happened, I said I'd fallen downstairs. I didn't want to get the police involved—there'd be some explaining to do as the cottage I'd been using was notorious.

Another danger in cottaging is that for the isolated and insecure gay man it fosters the idea that contact with other gay people is of necessity dirty, undignified, nerve-wracking and dangerous. It can do nothing for the self-image of those gay men who already have a bad opinion of their sexuality. Malcolm admitted that he didn't like being gay and he kept his homosexuality strictly confined to that small area of life which revolved around public lavatories. He never tried to see his contacts after the transient sexual contact was over. However, the beating prompted Malcolm to find other ways of meeting fellow gays. These other situations, in pubs and clubs, obliged him to talk. The different atmosphere and etiquette made him realise that there could be gay friendship as well as just sex. He still occasionally frequents the cottage ("old habits die hard" he says) and there is little doubt that it is easier for him to find sex there than it is in the bars and clubs, which revolve very much round the needs of younger people.

Indeed, cottaging remains a widespread phenomenon, and I have met couples who have got together in this way and gone on to develop rewarding and important long-term relationships. Nowadays, however, there are much safer ways of achieving that initial contact; the emergence of the gay movement in the Seventies brought with it a network of self-help groups and a commercial "scene" of pubs and clubs. This has mushroomed, and nowadays there is a myriad of choice in the gay world. The new-found confidence of gay people, and a recognition of their spending power, has also improved the quality of what is offered to them. Some of the larger pubs and clubs have international reputations. They are smart, fashionable and thankfully almost violence-free.

Indeed, they are being increasingly used by smart heterosexuals who recognise that they are superior to straight clubs.

Most large towns (and some of the smaller ones) now have a gay switchboard which can provide a counselling and befriending and information service for the emerging gay person. This can provide a safe and caring stepping-stone into the gay world.

You will find most of the switchboards, groups and commercial organisations listed in the gay magazines mentioned in the last section of this book. Find your nearest and give them a call. It could be your first step towards a whole new life.

If you're extrovert, fun-loving, quick to make friends and don't mind going into an unfamiliar pub on your own, then perhaps you only need to discover the whereabouts of your nearest gay local to put you on the road. But if you aren't the outgoing sort, or you need to build your confidence a bit before you throw yourself in, then one of the befriending groups could be the answer for you.

Making that initial contact can be a great stumbling-block for so many people; ringing a gay helpline for the first time may be their first deliberate approach to another gay person. Tom was nineteen when he saw a gay switchboard advertisement in his local evening paper. He wanted desperately to ring the number but was held back by fear of this first step:

> I cut the advertisement out of the paper and carried it round in my pocket for weeks. Every so often I would go to the phone with the intention of ringing, but couldn't bring myself to lift the receiver. I thought that somehow if I lifted the phone it would all be out— they'd be telling my parents and my friends would be able to see it written all over my face. You see, once I'd spoken to this gay switchboard, it would be real, it would exist somewhere else besides inside my head. I went on like this for ages until in the end I let it

connect. I don't know what I expected—someone
lisping and saying ducky I suppose—but the chap at
the other end was very reassuring about it all. It all
seems so exaggerated now, but at the time it was the
hardest thing I'd ever done.

Tom managed to get over the first hurdle where so many
others fall. In his conversation with the switchboard
volunteer, Tom talked about his home situation and what he
wanted from life. He eventually felt confident enough to go
along to a coffee evening which the group was holding. He
was met beforehand, so that he didn't have to face the
meeting on his own. Tom felt distinctly uncomfortable at the
first few meetings he attended. But he was surprised at the
variety of people he met and was also relieved to find he
could relax completely in this company:

I eventually got friendly with a few members of the
group and started going with them to other gay
places—a disco on Saturday and a pub a couple of
times. It was wonderful because I felt I belonged, and
because I knew that when I went to these events
anything could happen. I might find the man I'd been
hoping to meet for so long. I wasn't an alien in these
places, which was how I often felt when I was out with
my straight friends.

Many gays say that finding a social life with other gay people
is 'like coming home'—tension is lifted and all kinds of
opportunities for personal growth suddenly present
themselves. The sense of relief can be extremely exhilarating.
As Tom said: "I don't have to make excuses with these
people. I can look at who I want to, and I can tell them if I
fancy them, knowing that I won't get a smack in the mouth. I
can be myself at last and my life has changed completely."

Pubs and clubs

Years of reading about the "twilight world of homosexuals" in the straight press has probably produced an entirely untrue picture in the minds of isolated gay people. You've probably read of "sordid" pubs where men dress as women and drug pushers roam and dirty old men prey on young boys. Doubtless there are such establishments, but they are few and far between. Gay people demand a higher standard than that. You'll probably find the largest gathering of gay people locally at a gay pub. In the bigger cities such as Manchester and Birmingham, it isn't unusual to find gay discos attracting many hundreds of customers, especially at weekends. Such is the competition, that these places often provide cabarets and floor-shows as well as special "theme" evenings. The London clubs are famous for their extravaganzas and very professional shows.

Needless to say, night-clubs and discos aren't everyone's idea of a perfect evening's entertainment, but they are the major focus of gay social life. Pubs can vary widely in character, some being relaxed and quiet, others being rowdy with a heavy-laden sexual atmosphere. You might be lucky enough to live in an area where there is a choice.

Beware of easy answers

It's very easy, when first exploring the pub and club scene, to fall into the "cruising" habit (as searching for sex is termed). Try not to get into a routine which leads you to think that casual sex and uncommitted encounters are all that gay people can expect. However exciting it might appear, and however many opportunities there might be, most soon tire of the one-night stand roundabout. Far from providing an answer to loneliness it can, in fact, increase the sense of isolation in those who are already unhappy with their sexuality. There are health hazards, too, which we will explore later.

A lot of newcomers to the "scene" (and a few old hands) become disillusioned by the shallowness of it all and the problem of finding others who are interested in forming more substantial relationships. Some retire from the scene as soon as they have acquired a group of friends and are happy to stay within that small clique, entertaining in their own homes, using the commercial facilities only occasionally.

The personal columns of the gay press are filled with ads which say things like "Tired of the scene?" or "Need something more than discos?" This indicates a widespread desire for an alternative outlet to allow people expression of more than just their sexual urges. By all means enjoy the energy and excitement that goes with this new environment, but don't let the easy fun overwhelm your longer-term goals.

It's likely that you'll meet gay people who still have a lot of work to do on their feelings. Many still harbour the opinions about themselves which this book seeks to overcome. We need to help each other beat the fears that burden us. But be aware that your resolve to grow as a gay person can be very quickly undermined by others who are not happy with their own sexuality. They will produce all kinds of arguments to deter you. They seek, in a way, to justify their own refusal to change by trying to dampen down your determination. Many seek escape from their confusion by using alcohol and drugs to excess. Try not to fall into that trap. The best way to escape any pain that you are experiencing because of your sexuality is to face it and work on it—with a counsellor if necessary—and not try to cover it up with destructive palliatives like booze and drugs.

Physical isolation

Some gay people find their geographical location limits their opportunities. There may be no organised facilities for miles and this can be a serious drawback.

If you want to meet other people, one answer might be to move to another area. Drastic, maybe, but it could be the best way of exploring your full potential. Gays have always gravitated towards cities to find each other, and there is a big gay presence in every large conurbation. However, if you live in an isolated area and don't want to move away, it might be worthwhile starting a gay group of your own. It means hard work, but it has several advantages besides the obvious one of bringing you gay contacts. Being involved in starting and running a group obliges you to face, and think about, the many issues related to your gayness. And the very existence of the group has an effect on the local community—others can't pretend we don't exist if we show an organised presence.

To get the group started you have to find other people in your area to help out. The best way to do this is to let the gay press know that you intend to start a group and would like to hear from others in your locality. Obviously you'll need a contact point, and a phone number will be essential to start off with.

After you've got a small core of people together who are of a similar frame of mind (and it need only be two or three) you can think about where you want to meet. Groups throughout the country meet in members' homes (by far the cheapest and easiest of locations) or in church halls or pub rooms. Next, you have to find more members. This can be done by:

- Advertising in the local press. Often local papers have a "Community Notice board" feature, and will include your group's contact number if you ask them. Alternatively, the classified personal ads are quite cheap. Not all newspapers will accept this kind of advertising, of course, but if they do reject your application, write to the editor and complain. If this does not work, you could approach one of the campaigning groups and ask them for support.
- Putting up posters, perhaps in the library or community centre, or putting postcards in newsagents' windows.
- Make sure your existence is known to the local helping agencies like The Samaritans and social services. They'll refer people to you.
- Getting announcements made over any community programme put out by local radio stations. They might even invite you on to do an interview.

The person whose phone is being used as the contact point should be prepared for abusive and hoax calls. It isn't always easy to know when someone is having a joke at your expense by pretending to be gay. Experience can usually help you sort out the genuinely distressed gay caller from the person who thinks it's hilarious to "have you on". If there is any doubt, keep the caller talking without committing yourself. The hoaxer invariably cracks before long, either giggling or becoming abusive.

You might get threatening calls. The vast majority of these are meaningless, although frightening and unpleasant. It is sensible not to be too quick to give away addresses of meetings to people who call on spec. I have never known of anyone being seriously inconvenienced or put in danger by having their meetings infiltrated by gay-bashers, but in these days of rising violence you have to be a little security-conscious. Arrange to meet anyone who sounds even vaguely suspicious before giving out any addresses. The rendezvous should be in a well-populated public place: a shopping centre or cafe.

Everyone who shares the phone should be made aware that it is being made public as a gay helpline. It could be distressing all round if there were any misunderstanding. Even if you advertise restricted times when you want callers to ring, it is unlikely that these will be adhered to. An emotional crisis is no respecter of the clock and you can expect to get calls at any time of the night or day.

If you feel that you are getting out of your depth on any particular call (threats of suicide or special problems of which you have no knowledge) then ensure that you have another number to refer the caller on to. Many special interest groups are listed in the back of *Gay Times*.

If you find you enjoy this kind of work, you might like to consider taking some kind of training course in counselling that will help you be more effective. The large, well-established phone lines thoroughly train their members.

Please don't take on this kind of work unless you are committed to doing it properly.

One solution to the problem of "out of hours" calls, if there are enough funds available, is a separate phone line specifically for the gay calls. It can then be unplugged at times when no-one is around to answer it. If you are a really successful group you might even invest in an answering machine which could give an alternative number if you aren't available. Most exchanges have an inexpensive 'call-divert' facility which can automatically transfer calls to another number.

Once the group is established (and you're likely to find more than your share of obstacles along the way) it will function like just about any other community group, and how it develops will rest entirely with the membership. Quite often, though, the direction of the group is dictated by a small core of enthusiasts who are prepared to do the work. There is usually a mix of radicals who seek high visibility and those who are discreet and almost secretive. Several books dealing with the practical side of running a voluntary organisation will be available from your library.

Don't be put off by the sometimes quite ferocious opposition to the new group, often from religious sources. Facing critics can be an excellent way of strengthening your resolve to make a better life for yourself and, in the process, for other gay people.

Groups vary in character. Some put the emphasis on more gentle forms of socialising such as coffee evenings, visits to the theatre, cinema or pub. Others are political in nature and spend their time discussing gay issues and running campaigns. Mostly they're a mixture of both. The one thing that all the groups have in common is that they were started by ordinary gay people who recognised that if they didn't create social outlets nobody else would. It may seem a little ambitious for you at the moment, but it's an idea you can bear in mind when you're ready.

It takes courage to be open in a small town, and ultimately you have to decide on your own priorities. Which is most important to you: a full gay life or a rural existence? In the end, the need to relocate might be acute. Alternatively, if living somewhere like the Scottish Highlands or the Australian outback is important to you, then the sacrifice of being a long way from gay socialising might not be too big. There again, an advertisement in the personal columns of the gay press might bring a response from someone who would like to share your life in the wild or maybe even a neighbour you didn't know about. These ads are relatively cheap and might just do the trick. And, of course, dating agencies, pen-pal services and telephone introduction lines, the world wide web and Internet are all possible avenues of communication.

If you decide to try and contact people through personal advertising (and it's just as effective for those who are alone in the city as for those who are out in the country), please try to treat all your respondents with care. So often those who work on gay magazines are told by those who wrote in response to a personal ad that they received no reply. Although some of the people who write to you might not be what you had in mind, remember that they have taken a risk in putting pen to paper and revealing themselves to you. They probably did so in all sincerity. If you had done that you would expect at least an acknowledgement and a polite refusal; make sure you extend the same courtesy to others. And remember, photos are expensive, so please return any that are not of interest to you.

Another thing to remember when placing an ad—tell the truth. It's no use describing yourself as a twenty-one-year-old, handsome, well-muscled blond if, in fact, you are fifty, overweight and bald. Why say you are an affluent businessman looking for someone to accompany you on a world tour, when you are unemployed and penniless? Such fibs will certainly bring a response, but people will feel cheated when you aren't what you said, and you are likely to be humiliated and hurt by their reactions. So be honest, and take your chances. But be careful, too. Don't give your address on any response you send out, just a telephone number at first. Make sure that your contacts are genuine before you take them any further. And also bear in mind that there are some gay people around who will exploit any vulnerability which you display. I have met several gay men who have taken young men back to their homes, in all good faith, only to be robbed or abused in some other way. Don't be paranoid, but don't be silly about it, either. Loneliness can lead us to be too trusting because we want that human contact so badly. Be sensible, and good luck.

The Internet and worldwide web are other methods of finding friends and making contacts all over the globe. There are several chat and contact opportunities. If you're on the Internet and you want to access these, then you can use a piece of software called IRC (Internet relay chat). There are hundreds of "channels" or "chatrooms" on IRC, some of them very specialised. Ask your computer to search for just the ones with "gay" in the title. If you have a net connection with an on-line service provider, they will have provided you with the software as part of the package. You can visit a website and download the necessary software if you don't have it already. Try http://www.mirabilis.com. You can even connect up video cameras and have real face-to-face conversations with others who are similarly equipped.

If you do not have Internet access, consider using an Internet cafe. Some local libraries also provide access.

Wherever you go in the Western world you will find a network of gay meeting places, such as bars, clubs, coffee houses, book shops or groups, which will welcome you as a participant in the shared experience of being gay in a hostile world. Friendship is probably the most important element of a happy gay life. Work on it and treasure it.

5:Gay lifestyles and relationships

Gay lifestyles have changed considerably in the past few years. The gay community has matured, and although its self-examination continues, it has come to terms with the fact that there is no unique way of living that can be called *the* gay lifestyle; everyone who is gay creates their own. The coming of Aids has also radically changed the gay male outlook on life. After a period of fear-induced restraint, sex is back with a bang. Young people, brimming with a confidence unknown to previous generations of homosexuals, are freely exploring their sexuality, too. As well as confidence, this new generation has anger. They have been raised in a time when the threat of illegality does not hang so heavily. They cannot understand why they should be singled out for discrimination, and many of them are not prepared to tolerate it. They have become defiant, organising themselves into vigorous campaigning groups. Many have eschewed the traditional approach of lobbying and persuasion and have gone for all-out confrontation. Imaginative and courageous demonstrations have gained much publicity and raised public awareness of gay issues.

All this has led to factionalism within the gay community. There are those who will not compromise an inch in their pursuit of their own identity. They have applied the label "queer" to themselves in defiance of those who seek to use such a word as a poisonous insult. The radicals consider that only fundamental changes in the way we see ourselves will free us from our oppression. They often disparage the existing structures that gay people have built up, insisting that we are simply aping the lifestyles of our oppressors.

There are other gay people who prefer to be part of mainstream society, integrated and accepted. They prefer to take the more circuitous route of persuasion, trying to convince their straight friends that homosexuality isn't such a bad thing after all. They do not want to be part of a separate culture, but be assimilated into the existing culture on their own terms. They can be equally dismissive of what they see as extremists.

Other gays have married someone of the opposite sex, some refuse to have anything whatsoever to do with the gay community. We have gay people who are enthusiastic left-wingers and others who are equally eager to be right-wing. Some people lead a hedonistic life, others have devoted themselves to the welfare of others—e.g. working in the Aids movement. Some people manage to fit a bit of everything into their lives.

And so the gay community is developing, moving forward, becoming ever more diverse.

How we choose to live is very much a matter of personal inclination and opportunity; there are no pre-formed expectations as there are in the straight world. This opens up many possibilities, but also presents us with the problem of pinpointing exactly what our preferred lifestyle will be. For instance, a lot of gay people lead isolated lives not because they are happier alone, but because they are afraid of the consequences of entering into a committed relationship. Others involve themselves in a pair-bond because they think (and have been brought up to believe) that this is the "real way", even though it leaves them feeling frustrated and restricted. Pinpointing what we want from life can be tricky business; our needs may change with our circumstances. We can but try to get it right and be honest about our mistakes.

Living alone

For the purposes of this chapter we will consider living alone to mean living without a regular partner. Some people thoroughly enjoy living alone, actively avoiding any exclusive emotional commitment. They relish the freedom and make their decisions without reference to anyone else. They enjoy the ability to indulge themselves whenever and however they like. Ron is such an individual. He is a twenty-five-year-old bank clerk living near Birmingham:

> I don't have any desire to settle down and be part of a monogamous relationship. I have lots of friends and the nice thing is that I can see them whenever I choose. I'd hate to think that I can't meet new people or go to new places because my lover might not approve. I like to have absolute control of everything that happens in my life. I have the occasional sexual encounter, but no big romance. I like it that way at the moment, but I might change my mind if I meet the right person.

Others like the comfort of having a regular partner but not living in the same house. Bill is thirty-three and a teacher. He has tried living with other men but has found the experience cramping and irritating. He took the decision to live on his own after much thought:

> I enjoy my life at the moment. I've become used to having long periods by myself, and having someone around all the time makes me feel tetchy and argumentative. Nowadays I consider myself to be gregarious but essentially on my own. I do have a lover, Alan, but neither of us want to live in the same house. He spends the occasional night with me and I stay over with him sometimes. We like it the way we are. I'm not lonely, I like my own company.

There are many other gay people who consider themselves to be in a partnership but who choose to live separately from their lover. As long as both parties are happy with this arrangement, it has a lot to recommend it.

Living together

There are, of course, many gay men who want to make a full-scale partnership complete with a shared home, mutual responsibilities and commitments.

Paul and Desmond have a council flat in a large Northern town. They got the flat because the council has a housing policy which permits unmarried couples (and that includes gay couples) to go on the waiting list for suitable accommodation. Paul is a dustman and Des works in an engineering factory. Over the years they have been together they have made a successful home and have many friends. They make all important decisions in consultation with each other. Paul says:

> We both had a wild period before we decided to settle down. I think we wanted to try and sort things out before we took the plunge. Both of us enjoyed our earlier experiences but we were ready, when we met, to make a deeper commitment. I met Des at a gay group. We sort of fancied each other from a distance for quite some time before we actually got together. We found we had a lot in common. Both of us are from working class backgrounds and share the opinion that it is important to come out to our families, which we have both done. We now have this flat. It's only modest and it's in a tower block, but we are saving up the deposit for a small house.

Des was unemployed for a while soon after they moved in. I asked Paul how they had managed during that period, and he said:

Obviously, while I was the only one with a wage I had to subsidise him when necessary. He was getting his dole money so it wasn't so bad. If we wanted to go out together we could usually manage a drink or two or go to the occasional gay disco. Gay groups are a cheap way of spending a pleasant evening or two, although they usually end up down the pub afterwards. Des and I had made this commitment to each other, and simply because he'd lost his job through no fault of his own didn't mean I was going to change my feelings towards him. If you love someone you have to take the rough with the smooth. I love him very much, even after all these years.

Some gay people simply prefer to share a house with a group of gay friends. This has many advantages, the primary one being a supportive family when needed. It also has the usual disadvantages of communal living, like lack of privacy or difficulty finding space to be alone.

Settling down with "Mr Right"

The ways in which gay people choose to live are clearly many and varied. There are as many ways as there are gay people. From what I have gathered, though, most gay men harbour the dream (along with the majority of the rest of the population) that one day the right partner will happen along and that it will be possible to set up a home together.

Let's assume that you've met someone who seems to be your Mr Right and you think you can make a go of it together. How do you make sure it has the best chance of survival?

First of all, there is a great temptation to try and keep it "discreet" or completely secret from everyone else. Quite possibly even best friends don't know it exists, or if they do, they feel they mustn't mention it for fear of "causing offence". In other words, the relationship, with all its potential importance to the emotional well-being of both parties, is denied. What partners in such a closeted relationship are saying is that they are ashamed of their love. The result is to undermine and trivialise it. In such a vacuum where spontaneity must be smothered, the relationship is doomed to failure. People who are newly in love, and remain in love, need to be physically close to each other, to have their love recognised and applauded. Look at young lovers everywhere, arm-in-arm, hand-in-hand, seeking reassurance through touch. Gay people who make these gestures in public might find themselves open to ridicule, disdain or even arrest. Gay couples who have no friends to recognise their relationship can find themselves under great strain. If you want your relationship to survive, you must first accept the basic validity of your sexuality and then your unassailable right to love. After that, you need others to recognise and support it.

It shouldn't be assumed that straight people "can't understand" gay love. Of course they can. The feelings, sensations and complications that go with being in love are very similar for everyone, whatever their sexuality; so let your straight friends into your secret. Much of the pressure can then be released and new avenues of support opened.

For some people, the attainment of a loving relationship lessens their will to keep up the pretence. For others, the opposite is the case and fear develops. The existence of the relationship means that issues which have been avoided so far have to be faced. Because the homosexual feelings at last have a physical reality, the possibility of exposure is increased. The warmth and contentment which should be welcomed is tempered by apprehension. The protective barrier which the lone homosexual can erect so successfully suddenly seems very fragile.

It's up to you to choose a positive reaction. You can decide to let your love flourish in the light, or you can shut it away and see it wither in the closet.

Family affair

If you've come out to your family already, it's less likely that they'll be shocked if you come home one day with a new partner. Parents generally have the interests of their children at heart, and if you conduct yourself with dignity, the family will eventually accept your situation.

There may be problems, of course. Just as parents are reluctant to accept their child's homosexuality in the first place, so they might resist this flesh-and-blood manifestation of it. This is not always obvious. All may seem well on the surface, with parents smiling and polite, but underneath there might be unease. Patience and persistence are needed here, and parents' doubts can be conquered with honesty and goodwill. After all, parents disapprove of a lot of heterosexual partnerings, too. And remember, if the going gets rough and your parents refuse to accept either your assurances or your lover, there are alternative sources of support outside your family. The same goes for gay friends who aren't lovers, and who are similarly rejected by family. If your family know about your sexuality, but you try to keep the reality of it away from them by never letting them meet your gay friends, then suspicion and fear will be the result. They will have heard terrible tales of the kind of people who populate the gay milieu and may be worried about who exactly it is you are associating with and what kind of influence is being exerted over you. It's natural that the unseen and the unknown will generate anxiety in those who love you. Clear away the mystery and misunderstandings that might surround your gay friends in the eyes of your parents. Do this by allowing your family to meet them. A lot of tension will be relieved in this way.

Making a commitment

After having made the decision to settle down, some gay people want to make a formal commitment similar to marriage. Indeed, some have actually arranged pseudo weddings. These ceremonies have no legal status in Britain but if, because of your religious convictions, it is important to have some kind of blessing for your relationship, it is possible to find sympathetic priests and vicars who can help out. The gay religious groups have ready-made ceremonies for those who want them. If you have no religious feelings, but still want to mark the beginning of your relationship, the Gay and Lesbian Humanist Association (address at the back of the book) will be able to assist you with non-religious ceremonies. If you decide on such a ceremony, why not make it a big celebration to which you can invite your friends and maybe even your family. (You can find more information about this in my book *Making Gay Relationships Work*—Other Way Press.)

When the decision to live together is made, however, the hard part begins. Living with another person can be a richly rewarding experience, but if you are gay there are added difficulties to making it work. For instance it might well not have the support of friends and family in the way that a marriage would. But it also has some advantages—the chief one being that there are no strict roles for a same-sex couple as there are for heterosexuals. One researcher said that gay relationships were based on the principle of "best friendship" rather than the traditional heterosexual power hierarchy. As a result, they were much more likely to be equal and balanced.

This is not to say that there will be no power struggles within the relationship. Adapting to a new life as a couple is difficult. Changes occur in the lifetime of the relationship that can throw us off balance because we just aren't expecting them. Our priorities alter, or our libido often calms down as time passes and we regard each other differently as the initial period of romantic and sexual experimentation cools.

Tasks will be shared according to skills and enthusiasms. There may be a need to negotiate the less pleasant and more mundane household chores, like taking out the rubbish or cleaning the toilet. And negotiation is a skill that is well worth acquiring. It helps you sort out differences in needs and opinions. If you can negotiate successfully you need not spend the whole time trying to manipulate and score points over each other.

Negotiation is most successful when it is practised regularly. Learn how to sort out differences without getting into destructive arguments that don't sort out the problem.

Decide beforehand what the subject of your negotiation is going to be (where you want to go on holiday, for instance, or who is responsible for cleaning the car) and then stick to it. Don't get side-tracked into discussing other areas of difference—leave that until you've sorted out the problem in hand. Don't go into a negotiation with the intention of "winning" because that isn't the point. The best result of a negotiation is for both parties to come out of it feeling that they've got something satisfactory, even if it isn't as much as they had originally wanted.

Don't try to negotiate when you are at the height of a screaming argument, and don't try to sort out big problems between you during a love-making session—even if they are about sex. It can do a lot of damage to your attitudes of intimacy with your partner if you come to associate love-making with uncomfortable and tense heart-to-hearts. Most of all, be truthful in negotiation, and be sensitive to your partner's feelings, even if the matter under discussion seems trivial to you. Small resentments can often inflate themselves into damaging differences if they aren't tackled early on.

Money matters

The question of finances is tricky, too. Unless you discuss these at an early stage, arguments will almost certainly arise. Perhaps one partner earns more than the other, or one has a job and the other hasn't. How are you going to decide what contributions each will make towards the shared expenses? Will you pool the resources or will you agree on proportionate amounts and keep the rest of your cash separately?

Although gay men have, on average, more spare money to play with than heterosexuals, we don't all find it easy to manage. Differing attitudes to money should be fully explored before any major commitments are undertaken jointly. In the first flush of love, for instance, it might seem like a dream to own your own house. After you've rushed into a joint mortgage you might find things aren't working out or that monetary responsibility just doesn't suit one of the participants. You could even think about making a legally binding agreement about all joint financial matters, so that if differences arise later you can both be secure. It might not seem very romantic, but it makes sense.

Expectations

Many a romance has begun in a blinding firework display of passion and lust, only to find out it isn't quite so spectacular when the smoke has cleared. His cutting wit, which might have struck you as so engaging at the start of the affair, might begin to sound like irritating sarcasm when you have to listen to it day after day. And the cute untidiness that was so attractive in your lover at the first meeting might strike you as simple scruffiness later on.

Although there is a widely-held belief that, as far as human relationships go, "opposites attract", research tends not to bear it up. The more you have in common with your proposed partner, the more likely your relationship is to survive. If you simply love classical music but he cringes at the sound of Beethoven, or he adores eating out, while you prefer simple food, plainly cooked (at home), then at some stage there will be conflict. These might seem like small points, but they may be indicators of a more basic difference in your approaches to life. Some of them will be negotiable but others won't. Areas ripe for fundamental disagreement include religion, politics and ethics. If you differ greatly in these important areas, the prognosis for your relationship isn't good.

Physical attraction is important to most of us, but so many gay people invent for themselves the "perfect" partner and then find him difficult to locate. Nor can they easily accept anyone who is less than the fantasy. This is well illustrated in the ads that appear in the personal columns of the gay press. Often advertisers will specify very narrowly defined physical types: they must have blond hair, big muscles, be well-hung, non-camp, into leather, clean-shaven... the list goes on and on. The odds against finding such a fantasy man are very long indeed. And even if the physical requirements are met, it doesn't guarantee you're going to hit it off together.

Fantasy can play an important part in our sexual activities, but we should know where to draw the line between fantasy and reality. Clinging to the "perfect man" ideal while allowing opportunities for real romance and happiness to pass by because they are offered by lesser mortals is thoroughly self-defeating. If you are absolutely determined that you will settle for nothing less than a motor-cycle riding, red-haired Brad Pitt look-a-like who is into S&M, then unless you are very lucky indeed, I fear you are saving up disappointment for yourself.

Quentin Crisp's fantasy revolved around being made love to by a "big, dark man". In order to satisfy the fantasy, it would have to be a "real" big, dark man (in other words, a heterosexual). By definition, a heterosexual man would not wish to make love to Mr Crisp and this provided a very effective barrier between Quentin and happiness.

Perhaps Quentin Crisp lumbered himself with the impossible dream as a means of escaping the frightening consequences of making a serious relationship. Make sure you don't do the same.

Monogamy or not?

Another decision which may present itself in a relationship is whether it is going to be sexually exclusive. Those who subscribe to the idea that non-monogamy is a desirable option would say that outside stimulation prevents the primary relationship becoming stale. And anyway, one person can't possibly fulfil all the needs of another. A survey of American homosexuals who were living in long-term partnerships indicated that by far the majority of them had had sex with someone other than their partner. It has to be said, though, that this survey was conducted before the Aids crisis.

Naturally, Aids should not prevent us expressing our sexuality. If we're sensible, we can still have a rich sexual life without putting ourselves at risk. Nor should we imagine that monogamy is 100% protection against HIV infection.

Another survey, carried out by Project Sigma in London, indicated that when gay men get into a committed relationship they are apt, after a while, to forget the safe-sex message and to begin having unprotected sex with their primary partner. For most people in such circumstances it seems to be a matter of trust. They are saying to each other, "I love you, and we've made a commitment. We don't have to bother with condoms and precautions when it's just the two of us." This may be romantic, but it isn't sensible unless you are both absolutely sure that you have not been infected with HIV at some point in the past and that neither of you is secretly having unsafe sex with other people.

It is important, if we do decide to be "unfaithful" to our regular partner, that we take every precaution. Read the chapter on safer sex.

The other problem which risks spoiling relationships, when outside sexual activity is involved, is jealousy. The old green-eyed monster has been the bane of many an otherwise successful partnership.

Of course, no-one can predict how a relationship will develop, whether time will make it stronger or whether it will disintegrate through lack of interest or changing needs. While many swear fidelity at the start of a love affair, they might find it appropriate to embark on another relationship when, at a later date, an opportunity presents itself.

Many gay men have reported that the sexual elements of their relationship have disappeared after a few years, and although their love and attachment grew stronger, they ceased to have sex. If relationships are to survive, it is this kind of change that has to be recognised, acknowledged and accepted. The inability to adjust to the changes which are an inevitable part of any partnership is one of the main reasons why they fall apart.

Monogamy is an important issue for many people and it's something which you should discuss with your partner beforehand in order to avoid unpleasant confrontations later.

How safe are we?

It's a sad and frightening fact that thousands of gay men are now carrying HIV, the virus which is thought to cause Aids. Many are totally unaware of their infection.

If you have recently met someone who is special to you, and with whom you wish to share your life, what should be your attitude towards HIV? What were your sexual histories before you met? Have either of you ascertained your HIV status through testing? What kind of sex can you safely share together?

The issues raised by this complication should not be avoided. Will you both be tested so that you can know how far your love-making can safely go, or are you going to avoid the tests (and several over a long period will be required to be absolutely certain) and satisfy yourselves with safer sex? These are hard decisions with many possible repercussions. The best thing is to find an Aids counsellor and talk it over with him or her. You can be taken through all the issues and be given an idea of what the consequences of any decision might be. In the end, though, the choice will be yours.

In the meantime, if there is any doubt at all in either of your minds, you MUST practise safer sex. It needn't be as restrictive as it sounds, and there are some exciting ideas in the chapter on gay sex.

Blaming homosexuality

Relationships—be they gay or straight—do not come with guarantees, and we should be prepared for things to go wrong from time to time. It's tempting, during periods of emotional crisis, to blame the failure on our homosexuality. "It would be so much easier to keep a partner if I were straight" is the cry often heard from gay men who have suffered a setback in their search for love. In reality, the problem is likely to be unreasonable expectations or lack of application. Beware, therefore, of making your sexuality the scapegoat for ordinary difficulties which everyone has to face.

And when things go wrong in a partnership, don't give up too easily. Don't be too quick to sing what one writer called The Gay National Anthem, the refrain of which goes "It's all over, let's call it a day, it isn't working out." Relationships need nurturing, patience, tolerance and compromise.

Finding our own way

What has been said in this chapter can only serve as a springboard for your own needs. It's up to each of us to find a formula that is right for us.

The hardest part is pinpointing what it is we really want. When we've crossed that hurdle—and occasionally it takes several attempts—we can go for our dream.

6: Gay sex

The pain and the pleasure, the agony and the ecstasy; sex can take us to the height of passion and to the depths of squalor. It can be a simple expression of lust or part of a loving coupling that has deep significance for those concerned. And it isn't always easy to know which is which.

The instinct to have sex is primitive and primary, and one which few people want to deny, and there is no reason why it should be denied. Don't listen to the glum voices of the doom merchants, Aids does not mean that sex is off the agenda for gay men. If we are well informed, we can still have an exciting and varied sex life without putting ourselves at risk.

We are learning more about HIV and how it spreads, and what steps we can take to avoid becoming infected by it. We can minimise the risks with a little thought, a small amount of caution and a consistent attitude to safer sex. All very straightforward, you might think—but things never seem to work out that way, and the evidence suggests that safer sex isn't always high on the list of priorities, even for well-informed gay men. Our rational voice says: "If gay men know the dangers, why do they continue to have unsafe sex?" It's a difficult and complex question, but one of the answers is a lack of self-esteem. We've already discussed the effects of the negative indoctrination which most gay people receive in their early, impressionable years. One of the purposes of this book is to try to help people recognise and challenge the self-hate that has been so carefully nurtured over the years. But it isn't easy, and there isn't much encouragement for us to feel good about being gay. That means we often don't respect our sexuality, leading some people to behave dangerously, not only towards themselves but towards their sexual contacts.

If you are feeling unhappy about any aspect of your sexuality, or you are uncomfortable about the way your life is going, you need to seek help. Work on the problems instead of compounding them with even more damaging behaviour. Don't allow yourself to fall into the trap of thinking your life is not worth saving. Instead, start considering ways in which it can be improved so that you value it and want to protect it. Help is at hand, in the form of counsellors who specialise in helping gay people. Often they are gay themselves. Some sources of gay counselling can be found at the back of this book. Counselling, though, shouldn't be seen as a short-term "fix"; you need to keep applying the knowledge you have learned.

Finding out about sex

Sex education is tragically thin on the ground, even for heterosexuals. For homosexuals it is practically non-existent. Despite attempts to restrict the mention of homosexuality in schools, it is gradually being accepted that it is a subject which cannot be ignored. We cannot wait for attitudes to change, we need to educate ourselves now.

You may come across Aids education campaigns sponsored by religious groups (these organisations usually disguise their true motives by giving themselves important-sounding but misleading names like "The National Family Campaign" or "Family and Youth Concern". The odds are that any organisation with the any combination of the words "national" and "family" in the title will be anti-gay). Their idea of safer sex is no sex at all, unless it's heterosexual and within marriage. Unless you have very strong religious feelings and actually agree with this approach, then it is wise to disregard such campaigns. They are likely to damage the way you think about yourself and not only spoil your enjoyment of the sex life you are entitled to, but to create all kinds of other destructive conflicts, too.

Practice makes perfect

Like any other skill, sex needs practice in order to get it right. Unlike learning the piano, most people need little encouragement to rehearse their sexual exercises! So, in an attempt to clear up some of the misunderstandings and fears which linger in the minds of the inexperienced, let's look at a few of the ways gay men make love.

Masturbation

It's probable that most people's first experience of sexual pleasure comes from exploring their own body. Masturbation (wanking, tossing off, jerking off) is the most universal of all sexual practices. It can, if necessary, be a quick release of pressing sexual urges, or it can be slow, lingering and indulgent. The nice thing about masturbation is that you have total control.

Masturbation is neither immoral nor dangerous and there are very few people who haven't done it at some point in their lives. However, the old superstitions which are still in circulation (the ones about going blind or mad) linger uncomfortably in the back of some people's minds. In Victorian times, horrendous anxiety surrounded the subject of masturbation, and doctors went to extreme and cruel lengths to discourage it among the young, even to the extent of having boys' foreskins fastened shut with rings, clasps or staples. It was also believed that good nutrition would dissuade the young from playing with themselves and, believe it or not, this is how the famous Kellogg's breakfast cereals came to be developed.

Be assured that masturbation cannot harm you physically or mentally. It is not "self-abuse", it's simply self-pleasuring. It costs nothing, doesn't generally involve any elaborate preparations and is available anywhere that's convenient. Discard any guilt you might have about enjoying your own body.

Another anxiety that some people have—particularly younger people—is that they are masturbating too much. Some young men masturbate three, four, five or even more times a day and feel that this will, in some way, harm them. Don't worry. In young men the sexual urge can be extremely pressing, and if no other outlet is available, masturbation is a perfect solution. If you need to do it several times a day, then rest assured that it won't do you any harm. Your body will tell you when you've had enough. It might be advisable to take a zinc supplement tablet occasionally, as the release of large amounts of seminal fluid can deplete the body's reserves. Other than that, fire away.

Masturbation techniques rest of course with the individual, and most people find the style that suits them best by a pleasant process of experimentation.

Solo sex is often accompanied by fantasies which can, at times, be outrageously inventive. Inside your head, absolutely anything can happen. Fantasies are a valuable adjunct to the enjoyment of your body, and the beauty is that no-one else can know about it unless you decide to tell: you can be as wild as you want to be. Sex fantasies are completely harmless and a lot of fun can be gained from occasionally acting out erotic dreams. However, if your particular turn-on is to create images in your mind of violence or harm to other people, then such fantasies should remain strictly inside your head.

Masturbation is often aided by the use of erotic toys, books, magazines or videos.

Sex with a partner

For the gay person the first sexual encounter with someone of the same sex can be a revelation; it generally follows a long period—sometimes decades—of anticipation and fantasising. Perhaps after years of fruitless "trying" with the opposite sex, the admission is finally made and long-desired gay contact is established. Such was the case with Bernard, who was twenty-five when he had gay sex for the first time:

I can hardly describe the relief when it actually happened. I think it was the happiest, most memorable day of my life. It was the day I'd been waiting for since I was a kid. And it wasn't just the sex—it was everything that went with it. The sexual act was a sort of confirmation that I was really gay, it resolved an awful lot of issues that had been troubling me. I'd had girlfriends before and been very fond of them, but when I tried to get physically close there'd be this awful tension which left me feeling depressed. It just didn't feel right at all. When I met Vince it was the exact opposite. I was walking three feet off the ground for the next week.

Such feelings of relief are often accompanied by a dramatic increase in self-esteem. Psychologists have accepted that these feelings of elation are less connected with the act of sex than with the way we see ourselves after it. A pleasant sexual encounter assures us that we are attractive, desirable and leaves us with a distinct sense of well-being.

So, what exactly do gay men do in bed?

It is almost infinitely variable. For some, closeness and affection are far more important than acrobatic sex, but briefly, the techniques which gay men use most often are:

Mutual masturbation, or wanking off together

This simply means stroking and manipulating your own or your partner's genitals. For many, this has proved a perfectly satisfying limit to their sexual needs. It has the advantage of being easy from a mechanical point of view, and one of the safest forms of safer sex. Of course it can be varied and enhanced in many ways—by the use of sex toys, kissing and cuddling and experimenting with lubricants.

In the USA "jerk circles" have been popular. In these, as many men as want to sit around masturbating together. It gives a communal sexual outlet without putting any of the participants in danger of acquiring HIV. Such activities would be completely illegal in Britain.

Fellatio or cock sucking

Also called "sucking-off" or a "blow-job", it means sucking your partner's penis. When this is done mutually it's called "sixty-nine". In fellatio it is important not to cut or scratch the penis with your teeth. The human mouth contains many potentially harmful organisms, so it is important not to break the skin. A little gentle practice will help you get this right. Unless specifically requested, it is also polite to present your partner with clean genitals.

There are lots of positions for fellatio, and with imagination you can have a great deal of fun discovering your own favourite. Sometimes the muscles in the mouth can get a little tired if it goes on for a long time, but I can't think of a pleasanter way of getting face-ache.

Some people also like to cover their partner's cock in their favourite food and then suck and lick it off. Jam, whipped cream, ice cream or Bovril have never tasted better and have never been so enthusiastically eaten!

The health risks attached to sucking are not clear. Resist unprotected sucking if you have sores or cuts in your mouth, and withdraw before "coming". However, if you like to swallow your partner's ejaculation, make sure your mouth is healthy and that you don't have an ulcer. The acids in the stomach will kill HIV once the sperm gets down there.

If you want to be absolutely safe, use one of the widely-available fruit-flavoured condoms. Perhaps these would be more popular if they tasted of cock rather than strawberries—after all, you can eat fruit salad any time. When cock sucking, try not to choose condoms that are treated with spermicide—the chemical can cause sore throats for some people.

Frottage or rubbing

Rubbing your bodies together for mutual pleasure is, again, a safer method of safe sex for gay men to enjoy. With no penetration there is very little likelihood of HIV being transmitted. Once again, there is great scope for improvisation: erotic massage, exotic and acrobatic positions, rubbing unlikely parts of your bodies together. Playing with lubricating oils can lead to the discovery of wonderful sensations, and can also help avoid "friction burns" on sensitive parts of the anatomy.

There is no reason why you should not simulate intercourse by fucking your partner between the legs, under the arm or wherever else your explorations take you, so long as it does not involve penetration of the anus. If rubbing your penis between his buttocks, beware that accidental penetration does not occur.

Body rubbing offers a lot of scope for variety. You can stimulate each other in all kinds of situations, in and out of clothes, and the possible combinations of two bodies is almost endless. Happy frottage!

Anal intercourse, fucking, bumming or buggery

This involves one partner putting his cock into the arse of the other and thrusting. It is a practice frequent among heterosexuals, too, either because no contraception is available or simply as a variation.

Anal intercourse is the sex act most associated with the transmission of HIV. It has been shown repeatedly that by far the majority of gay people who have acquired HIV, did so through anal fucking. It is wise, therefore, to think very carefully before embarking upon it with anyone, unless you are absolutely certain of their health. Remember that people who have been infected with HIV are often unaware of the fact. They may appear healthy, but they are still capable of transmitting the virus.

Perhaps the most valuable piece of advice you can have is to drop anal intercourse from your sexual repertoire, unless you are absolutely certain of your partner's HIV status. There are so many safer alternatives, so many wonderful erotic experiences you can share without putting each other at risk.

Nevertheless, it can't be denied that fucking is a very appealing activity for many gay men, and most will want to try it at some time. If you are absolutely determined to fuck, then use a rubber sheath (Durex, condom or French letter). This is by no means a 100% protection, but it's better than doing it without any protection at all. Sheaths cannot guarantee safety, and many things can go wrong: they can come off quite easily, they can split and a significant proportion have been shown to leak. Many gay men are insufficiently familiar with condoms and find them cumbersome and annoying. It is just too easy in the heat of the moment to discard the condom once the decision has been made to engage in intercourse.

Here are a few guidelines for the use of sheaths:

- Ensure it has a BSI Kitemark as an assurance of quality.
- Do not use a sheath after the date marked on the packet.
- Don't inflate the condom to test it for holes as doing so will weaken it.
- Use a new sheath every time.
- Don't tear the packet open with your teeth. Open it carefully so there is no danger of tearing the sheath inside.
- As soon as the penis goes hard and erect, the sheath should be unrolled onto it.
- If the sheath does not have a teat on the end to catch the semen, ensure that you leave about half an inch at the end of the sheath for this purpose.
- The sheath can be torn by rings and sharp fingernails, so be careful.
- After love-making, the penis should be pulled out of your partner before it becomes soft, with the sheath held

firmly in position at the base of the penis. Take care not to spill any semen.
- Dispose of the sheath carefully down the toilet, wrapping it in toilet paper to ensure it flushes away.

I repeat that the use of condoms is not 100% safe, but it is certainly better with than without. Remember also that Vaseline and other oil-based lubricants (Crisco, baby oil, cooking oil, butter etc.) will melt the sheath, so only use KY, 1-2-3 or some other water-based lubricant (there are plenty now on the market in sex shops etc., but many of them are vastly overpriced and don't work any better than KY, which you can get from any chemist). And when lubricating, try hard not to get KY inside the condom—this just makes it more likely to slip off.

There is resistance to condoms because some gay men think they interfere with the pleasures and sensations of fucking. One man described it as "like sunbathing with a raincoat on." But a small reduction in sensation is small price to pay for the peace of mind it brings. The best way to familiarise yourself with condoms is to buy a packet (and as well as in chemists and public toilets, they're now widely available in garages, record shops, and so on). Play around with them in one of your wanking sessions. Some men actually find the foreplay involved with putting condoms on themselves or their partner to be very exciting. Eroticise condoms in your own mind, and they'll become an intrinsic part of your sex life. You can help the process along by leaving packets around where you might need them at short notice—on the bedside table, in your wallet or wherever they would be easily accessible in the heat of the moment.

Oral/anal sex, rimming or licking

Anilingus, as rimming or tonguing the arse is also called, holds a strong appeal for some gay people. It holds the same place in gay sex as licking their partner's cunt does for heterosexual men.

If you want to go ahead, ensure that your partner is as clean as possible (by its very nature, that part of the body can never be totally hygienic) and that your mouth is free of sores and cuts. You might wish to employ a dental dam/oral sheath/oral dam—a sort of condom for the tongue—which allows you to use your tongue without it coming into direct contact with whatever it is you're licking. Dental dams take a bit of practice, but might save a lot of problems if rimming takes your fancy. They would reduce the HIV risk and also provide protection against hepatitis A and B, both of which can be acquired by this activity.

Fingering or finger-fucking

One or more fingers are inserted into the anus, either by your partner or by yourself. It's a common means of stimulation used by gay men and can provide an exciting adjunct to masturbation. The anal region has many nerve-endings which produce erotic sensations when stimulated. The prostate gland (part of our internal sexual equipment which can be accessed through the anus) can be massaged for extra pleasure. If you are doing it to your partner, or he is doing it to you, you might want to be extra cautious by using a condom over your finger(s) or even wearing disposable surgical gloves. Always ensure that your finger-nails are cut and filed down with no ragged edges and that you aren't wearing any rings with sharp edges. Use lubricants to ensure that you don't hurt your partner—the area is ultra-sensitive to pain as well as pleasure.

Sex toys

Sex toys are popular, and easily available. The designs for some of these are far from new, having been mentioned in the sex manuals of ancient India and China. Dildos or false penises have always been popular, and as long as they are kept clean and for the use of one person only, can be very pleasurable. Avoid the giant varieties which might seem exciting but can actually be quite dangerous: steer clear of anything more than ten inches in length. There are double-headed dildoes that can be used by both partners at once—it's almost impossible for these to get lost inside you. Vibrators, too, can happily be used either solo or with a partner. If you've never come across a vibrator before, it is a plastic or rubber phallus-shaped appliance equipped with batteries which cause it to vibrate very rapidly when switched on. If you insert this into your anus it can intensify your orgasm by massaging the prostate. Use adequate lubrication with these devices, don't try to use them dry. Spit is not enough.

Ensure anything you put in your anus is smooth and without sharp edges; if you insert a dildo, vibrator or other object (banana, bottle, courgette—you name it, someone's tried it) be very careful not to lose it; if it goes all the way in it might be difficult to retrieve. If this happens to you, then seek medical attention immediately. It's no time to be shy, and you'd be surprised how many times this particular problem crops up in hospital casualty departments.

Another sex toy is the suction device which is used for mechanical fellatio. They can be fun, but don't believe any claims that they can increase the size of your penis, they can't. And don't fall for any other promise in that direction, there are no creams or exercise regimes that can make your genitals bigger. The people who sell such ideas are well aware of men's anxiety over size. Although there is a great emphasis on size in the gay world, it doesn't mean that those with average-sized equipment can't have a good time. There are just as many pleasure receptors on the head of a small penis as there are on a giant one. Mr Bigdick doesn't get any more pleasure from his ding-a-ling than Mr Diddy-dick does. Quality is more important than quantity in the end. What use is a foot long cock if you don't know what to do with it? Sexiness is an attitude of mind, not a giant bulge in your trousers.

Whilst we're on the subject of artificial suction devices, please be very careful if you're experimenting with vacuum cleaners. There have been some horrendous accidents among men who have tried to simulate a blow job with the Hoover.

If worries about size are really affecting your sex life, there are operations available now which claim to be able to make the cock bigger. One of these involves injecting fat from another part of the body into the penis to give it more girth, while another brings out some of the shaft that is concealed inside the body. Neither operation carries any guarantee of satisfaction, but both can pose considerable risks.

You might also come across cock rings. These are leather or metal devices which are placed around the balls and over the top of the penis when it is soft. After you get an erection, the ring stops the reverse flow of blood which maintains the erection longer. There is little danger from these pieces of equipment so long as they aren't worn for too long and aren't too tight.

Fantasy

Fantasy games are also in vogue as an alternative to more conventional forms of sex. Master/slave scenes can be acted out by those who are excited by such ideas. Uniforms and fetishistic clothes made from leather, rubber, Lycra, denim and corduroy can also provide a lot of entertainment, if they particularly turn you on. Some people find jock-straps irresistible, while others are ecstatic about workmen's clothes and hard hats.

Sado-masochism (S&M) is an area that appeals to some, although not as many as one might think, and there are countless books that can explain this in more detail. However, the 1990 case of Operation Spanner has thrown the whole area of sado-masochistic sex into a legal muddle. Several men were jailed for having consenting S&M sex. At present it is probably wise to be discreet about your activities in this area. Don't write things down, or keep videos, photographs or any other record of your pleasures. These may be used in evidence against you at a later date, as they were against the men in the Operation Spanner case.

If you are secretly turned on by the idea of making love to a policeman in his uniform, why not get you partner to pop along to the fancy dress hire shop and act out your dream in the bedroom (or kitchen or broom cupboard)? If the prospect of sex with a sailor or soldier excites you, why not pay a visit to an ex-army clothes shop—and make your fantasy come true?

Using the bathroom and shower can open up many avenues and a lot of fun can be had by looking round the house for items that can be used in erotic games. Friends have reported employing step-ladders, egg-beaters, rocking chairs, cling-film, custard and vegetable oil in their experiments. One even told the story of how he was leaning out of the bedroom window, holding a conversation with the next door neighbour, while his lover was on the floor, out of sight, fellating him at the same time.

If you are experimenting with any activity which involves asphyxiation, be extremely careful. The number of deaths each year of people trying these things is tragic and there are no fool-proof ways to protect yourself from things going wrong. Be very wary of people you don't know tying you up or handcuffing you. Once more, bitter experience has shown that sex can lead us into dangerous territory, and in 1992 a serial killer used these methods to disable his gay victims before murdering them. Trust is the key word in many sex games, so make sure you know something about your partner before you embark on anything that you don't have complete control over.

Male rape

A recent survey by Project Sigma found that rape is also far more common among gay men than was originally thought. A high proportion of participants in the survey revealed that they had been forced to have sex against their will at some stage in their life. If this has happened to you, consider ringing one of the gay counselling agencies for help. The same principles apply as with male-female assault. If a person says "no", then that refusal should be accepted—no matter at what stage the love-making has reached. Even if you are naked in bed together, you should still have the right to withdraw from the activities if you want to.

There is no excuse for coercing people into having sex against their will; it is a violation of their human rights and a humiliating experience which might cause them lasting damage. Because many gay men like "rough sex" it may be difficult for your partner to know when your protests are real and when they are "part of the game". If you feel that things might get wild and rough, agree with your partner a signal beforehand that will let him know if it's going too far. Often the thing that has attracted us to someone is their strength and large build. We must understand that if we are having sex with a stranger who is substantially stronger than we are, the risk is always present that they will abuse their power over us.

You do not have the right to force people into unwanted sex, and no-one has the right to force you.

Those who have been subject to this kind of abuse are often understandably reluctant to go to the police, but some forces are making efforts to deal more sensitively with this issue. The law, too, has been changed to recognise the serious consequences of male rape, and it is now treated in the same way as the rape of a woman by a man.

If an experience of rape has caused you more stress and anxiety than you feel you can handle alone, please seek help from one of the agencies specially dealing with sexual abuse.

Safer sex

The Terrence Higgins Trust, a charity whose aims include the dissemination of accurate information about Aids and HIV infection, says: "The evidence clearly shows that the greater the number of men you have unsafe sex with, the greater the risk of your catching the virus, and the virus is spread most commonly by anal intercourse. These are the clear facts."

So what is safer sex? As a simple rule of thumb, it means sex that does not involve inserting part of someone's body into someone else's or does not include the exchange of bodily fluids.

The more people you have unsafe sex with, the more often you expose yourself to new risks. If you are having sex within an absolutely monogamous relationship which existed before 1980, and neither of you have injected drugs using shared equipment, then you are probably safe with any sex act, as far as HIV transmission is concerned.

The only limit placed on the kinds of sex any couple can have is that dictated by their imagination and desires—and the safer-sex guidelines, of course. Nowadays ingenuity and inventiveness have been applied to the creation of alternatives to fucking.

Boozers beware

If you have resolved to protect yourself from Aids, then you should bear in mind the factors most likely to undermine your chances of success. First, there is alcohol. All our good intentions can be thrown out of the window when we have had too much to drink: inhibitions are down and we can become extremely irresponsible. Remember, alcohol is a mind-altering drug and nobody is immune from its effects. When under the influence we can find ourselves behaving in ways we wouldn't dream of doing when we're sober. Never allow alcohol to tempt you into putting your life in danger by breaking your determination to avoid a brush with HIV. This is easier said than done. When we are tipsy and an opportunity for sex presents itself, our judgement can be grossly impaired. Only by dogged determination and an iron will can we overcome the dangers of alcohol-induced foolishness. Perhaps if you're out with friends you could resolve to remind each other to Play Safely if it seems that drink and sex are going to be bed-partners. And make as many preparations as you can in advance. Have condoms in your pocket, on your bedside table or wherever else you feel you might need to reach for them at short notice. Don't put the responsibility onto the other person, make sure you have the johnnys with you at all times.

Lack of confidence

Another obstacle is the sheer inability to communicate our needs and wishes to a prospective partner. If you have agreed to a sexual encounter with someone who then assumes it will include anal intercourse, how do you say "no"? For the inexperienced this can be a real dilemma. You are anxious to enjoy the encounter and are reluctant to put it in jeopardy by imposing restrictions. So how do you tell your partner that you aren't prepared to be fucked?

You might have met the most beautiful man in the world, and you might be bursting with lust for him, but you must not let that intense desire smother your common sense. Many of us find that doing sex is much easier than talking about it, but we really should make an effort to set out the limits before we begin. Try to approach the preliminaries in a positive way, by emphasising what you will do rather than what you won't. Some people are turned on by dirty talk, while others find it excruciatingly embarrassing. Unfortunately there is no easy way round this. Hopefully any prospective partner will be equally anxious not to take any risks and may well be relieved by your taking the initiative. Remember, if anal sex is put off limits there is still plenty of opportunity for a wild erotic encounter which can be enjoyed to the full in the knowledge that neither of you is going to put your health on the line. Once again, low self-esteem can cause gay people to disregard safer sex. If you are living dangerously, then you should think carefully about getting help to tackle the underlying problems.

Intense research is being conducted into all aspects of Aids and HIV infection, but there is unlikely to be a cure for some years to come. Despite success with combination therapies to treat HIV once it has been acquired, there is little progress being made in the production of a vaccine that will prevent infection in the first place.

Only consistent changes in the behaviour of gay men will halt the spread of this ghastly illness in our community. There is more information about HIV in the next chapter. Make sure you read it.

The dangers of "on-line thinking"

Aids educators have made valiant efforts to tell us all about safer sex, to present it attractively and to encourage us to make a habit of it. However, the concept of safer sex is a relatively recent invention and is often hard to reconcile with something as primitive as sex. It is rapidly becoming apparent that although gay men might now have absorbed the theory of safer sex, many of them are finding it difficult to practise it consistently in their own lives. The Public Health Laboratory Service has been monitoring reports of gay men who have tested negative once and then subsequently tested positive. In 1988 there were 25 such cases, by 1990 there were 82, while in l994 the number had risen to 139. This indicates that some men are finding it difficult to make safer sex a hard and fast rule. Knowing the facts is no guarantee that gay and bisexual men will be unwavering in their commitment to safer sex.

One man who has studied this phenomenon is the Australian researcher Ron Gold. He recruited gay men who were having anal sex despite knowing the risks they were taking, and asked them to keep a diary of their sexual activities. He concluded that there are two ways that gay men think about unprotected anal sex. He called them "off-line thinking" and "on-line thinking". Off-line thinking is the kind that is open to rational persuasion and argument, when your mind is in off-line mode it accepts the safer sex message. But on-line thinking is the kind that happens quite on the spur of the moment. The writer Keith Alcorn made this analogy for on-line thinking in an article in *Gay Times*: "It's the kind of logic which tells you you can run across a dangerous, busy road to save you walking the extra ten yards." And it's also the kind of logic that gay men can use to justify fucking without a condom—even when they know very well the risks they are taking. If you've ever had sex which you knew to be unsafe, ask yourself if you've ever used any of these excuses to justify your action:

- "He's young and healthy—he couldn't possibly be infected"
- "He's promised to pull out before he comes, so it'll be OK"
- "I've always taken precautions in the past—just this once will be all right"
- "I've had unprotected sex with him before, so if he's got HIV it's probably too late anyway"

These spurious rationalisations are common, and it's obvious that unprotected sex is far more frequent than we'd like it to be. If you find yourself backsliding in your efforts to avoid HIV infection, then remember that there are many others also struggling. Think carefully about the self-justifications that you might be using for relaxing your vigilance, and try to challenge them when you find yourself thinking "on-line". No-one wants to spoil the spontaneity of sex, but there's no reason, as we'll see, that sex can't be enjoyed in relative safety. Challenge yourself to think "off-line" when you're cruising or bedding your latest partner.

A time and a place

It's nearly always better if you can enjoy sexual encounters in warm, comfortable and safe surroundings. Naturally there will be occasions when an extra thrill can be gained from an alfresco episode, but these should be cautiously arranged. Gay men sometimes meet each other in dangerously "public" places, and on such occasions the sex has to be hurried and can be spoiled by the fear of discovery. In these often impersonal circumstances it is much more likely that thoughts of safer sex will be discarded.

A good start to your love-making is to ensure that you are in a private place where you won't be disturbed. Anxiety can produce "performance difficulties" such as impotence, which we will discuss later. When you are ensconced in your love nest, take time to touch and explore each other and enjoy the warmth and closeness. Many gay couples spend literally hours kissing and cuddling each other before they move on to the more genital-centred activities. But, of course, the genitals are not the only erotically charged area of the body—the nipples, ears, buttocks, navel and even the feet can give an extra dimension to love-making.

Here again, some gay men cannot regard what they do as love-making. The only way they can cope with the self-loathing they feel is to see it as "only sex". For such people there must be no preliminaries—no kissing or signs of affection. If this is the way you feel then you may have some work to do on your attitudes. A little counselling would go a long way to helping you confront the issues which deny you the health-promoting benefits of touch and closeness. Loving touch, according to researchers, is immensely important for the reduction of stress and anxiety. The reassurance of a tender touch is a therapy worth a thousand tranquillisers, and anyone who is accustomed to regular physical closeness will tell you how desperately they miss it when it isn't around.

Try to tell your partner what you want from him. Verbalising sexual needs is not always easy, but it can help to avoid much of the resentment which arises when one partner always obliges his lover, but never feels satisfied himself. Encourage your partner to say what he wants, and don't be reluctant to express which particular activities you find exciting and which turn you off. There is much fuel for dissatisfaction unless partners can bring differences and unfulfilled desires to each other's attention.

Sexual difficulties

From time to time sexual problems arise which threaten both the relationship and the confidence of the sufferer. The main culprits are erection difficulties and poor ejaculation control. Impotence (the inability to maintain or retain an erection) is something which most men experience at some time. Usually it is a temporary phenomenon and disappears with a little patience.

"Situational impotence" is the name given to the occasional droop that men experience when they find themselves in circumstances that are stressful. Such circumstances might be:

- **A threatening environment**. Those who seek partners in cottages and have sex in surroundings where there is a high risk of discovery, have a great deal of anxiety to contend with. This often leads to the inability to get an erection.
- **Fear of being unable to perform**. For gay men who are in the habit of picking up strangers for sex, there is a constant pressure to perform "on demand". The body won't always comply, and after a few non-starts, when erections don't materialise or can't be maintained, a fear of "failure" or being derided leads to impotence.
- **Too much drink or drugs**. Over-indulgence can lead to erection failure as it tends to depress the senses.
- **Unhappiness with sexual orientation.** An individual's basic inability to accept his homosexuality can be the cause of impotence. This is often a deep-rooted problem and counselling may be of help.
- **Lack of interest in partner**. Some gay men find it difficult to say "no" to sexual advances, even when they aren't actually interested. This reluctance to refuse offers of sex can be connected with low self-esteem or a lack of confidence and can also be helped with counselling.

With a little pre-planning it is possible to avoid all these circumstances, and the problem quickly rights itself. The most important thing to remember, if you are experiencing a period of erection failure, is not to panic. It is, in most cases, a temporary psychological block. Becoming anxious about the prospect of the next failure will simply ensure that such a failure occurs. Try to accept the temporary lapse and reassure yourself that it will right itself in time.

For some men, though, there is a long history—often going back to early childhood—of sexual humiliation and maltreatment. This can create a chronic impotence which the American sex researchers Masters and Johnson called "primary impotence". The sufferer may have felt sexually inadequate for a long time, and it may have interfered with emotional development. Such cases can be treated. If you think this might apply to you, seek expert help. Nearly all sex therapists recognise the importance of homosexuality as a part of the human experience and will treat their gay clients with the same understanding as they do their straight ones. You need not fear shock or censure. And if you're lucky, you might even find a gay therapist who may find it easier to empathise with your difficulties.

If the impotence you are experiencing has developed within a stable, loving relationship, you need to ask some questions of yourselves. Is everything satisfactory in other areas of your life together? Are there hidden conflicts which need to be aired, explored and resolved? Once again, a counsellor could help you pinpoint and clear up these conflicts. Now there is also the option of Viagra, an effective anti-impotence drug which has been developed to apparently great effect.

Because each individual tablet of the drug (chemical name sildenafil) is quite expensive, there has been some controversy over whether it should be available on prescription under the NHS. If it becomes so, then its availability will not be restricted only to heterosexuals. The Department of Health has made clear that it would be prescribed to anyone for whom the doctor thinks it is appropriate.

If you are having erection problems, and you think that Viagra might help, then don't hesitate to contact your GP and ask his opinion.

Viagra is also being touted as a recreational sex drug, allowing more frequent and longer-lasting erections. The tablets may become as easily available on the gay club scene as Ecstasy. However, there is evidence that Viagra should not be taken at the same time as poppers (akyl nitrite) as, according to *Aids Treatment News*, the interaction of the drugs can cause dangerously low blood pressure.

But before rushing to embrace Viagra as a recreational drug, we should look beyond the hype and recognise that this substance is not a cure-all for sexual problems. It may overcome the symptoms, but not necessarily the underlying problem.

Viagra has also been shown to have side effects for some men. There have even been reports of fatalities, although these are rare. If Viagra really does produce the benefits that its manufacturers claim, then gay people who need it should not hesitate to take advantage of it.

Ejaculation problems

Ejaculating or "coming" too soon can spoil a sexual encounter—it's over before it has really begun. People who feel this is a problem for them often despair of ever enjoying a prolonged sexual episode.

First we have to decide what we mean by "coming too soon". Just as some men have faster reflexes, others find that a climax follows very soon after stimulation begins. It could be that after a prolonged abstinence from sex, excitement can be so intense that a climax is reached almost before you've started. This just needs a little time to correct itself. But after a few such experiences, a man can condition himself into expecting it to happen every time. And because he is expecting it with such dread, lo and behold, it happens. A pattern is soon established.

Don't talk yourself into believing that this is a tragedy—in most cases it is quite simple to correct. But do discuss this problem with your lover so that both of you understand what is happening; as always, the best way to tackle it is with the help of a warm, loving partner. Together you could try the "squeeze technique" also developed by Masters and Johnson. It's a very simple treatment, ideal for self-application:

We'll consider it as being applied by partner B to partner A who has the hasty ejaculation problem.

Once again, you should be in a comfortable situation where you won't be disturbed. Partner B sits with his back against the wall or headrest of the bed with his legs apart. Now Partner A sits between B's legs, so that his back is touching

B's chest. B then reaches round and fondles A's genitals until A has an erection. As soon as A feels the ejaculation approaching, he tells B, who takes the head of A's penis between his thumb and forefinger and squeezes it quite hard for three seconds. The pressure should be applied just below the corona—the "cap" of the penis where it meets the shaft. This will result in not only stopping the ejaculation, but also in the loss of most of the erection. The process is repeated as many times as can be managed (within, say, half to three quarters of an hour). On the first occasion usually about four or five squeezes are managed before the ejaculation takes place. After a few sessions, the period of time between stimulation and ejaculation lengthens until eventually full control is regained.

Obviously this can be quite frustrating for the helping partner, so his needs should not be neglected, and there is no reason why A should not fulfil a "service" role for B until the therapy is completed.

The best way to prevent the onset of these problems is to try and avoid the situations that create them. You should also increase your knowledge of the way your body works. There are hundreds of books available about sex—nearly all of them aimed at heterosexuals—but from which you can still learn useful things. An increasing number of gay sex manuals and videos are appearing and they can be very reassuring. You might want to start with my *A-Z of Gay Sex* (The Other Way Press) or Peter Tatchell's *Safer Sexy* (Freedom Editions). Arm yourself with knowledge and it can be good protection from the fears that can lead to impotence and premature ejaculation.

To summarise:
- Beware. Some way-out sexual practices—like introducing the whole fist or forearm into the rectum (fist-fucking)—can be deadly.
- If you have deep-rooted problems which stand in the way of your enjoying sexual experiences, don't hesitate to

get help from one of the counselling agencies or a sex therapist. Don't be embarrassed—they're there to help you.

• Experimenting sexually with your partner can be exciting, but never be coerced into situations you don't want. Learn how to say "no", but also learn how to say what you do want from sex. Safer sex is not only about what you can't do, it's also about the wonderful things you can do. Fetishes and fantasies are harmless, so long as everyone involved in them is happy.

• Try not to always regard sex as a solely genital experience—it can be greatly enhanced by emotional involvement.

• Think very carefully before engaging in anal intercourse, but if you are determined to go ahead with it, use a condom and plenty of water-based lubricant. Anal intercourse is the primary means of acquiring HIV.

• Masturbation is a wonderful alternative—make full use of it. To quote a famous phrase from a safer-sex leaflet: "Wanking—go for it!"

The "no sex" alternative

Aids has made most gay men rethink their approach to sex, and some have decided to eliminate genital sex entirely from their lives—to become celibate. This may seem a drastic solution, but for a few people it is a feasible alternative. Our opponents would love us to believe that celibacy is the only answer to Aids, but, as we've seen, it isn't so. It is possible to enjoy all the benefits that spring from sex without harm to ourselves or other people. If you don't feel that a life without sex is right for you, then don't be pushed into it by either guilt or fear of disease.

Given all we've said about the health-promoting value of sex, is a celibate lifestyle likely to have adverse effects on our health?

Dr Alan Riley, a specialist in sexual medicine and co-editor of *Sexual and Marital Therapy* has been quoted as saying:

"We can't say a regular sexual outlet is essential to health. But if people have a sexual appetite, it can make them frustrated or aggressive to suppress it." It is true that the longer you go without sex, the less you crave it. Conversely, satisfying desire tends to stimulate fresh desire.

If you feel that celibacy is right for you, then there is no reason why you shouldn't opt for it. If you want to succeed, it is perhaps useful to have something challenging and demanding in your life to use up the energy that would otherwise be used in sexual activity.

Being celibate does not necessarily mean being lonely. Not having sex doesn't mean you are debarred from having intimate, loving relationships with other people. And if circumstances change, so can your approach to sex.

7: Gay health

Aids and HIV have fallen out of media fashion. At one stage, the newspapers were full of doom and gloom about the epidemic, but now we rarely hear the topic mentioned. For most people, the news that new drugs have been developed that appear to be containing the virus, means that Aids has become a non-issue for those not affected. TV coverage now seems to be concentrating more on the devastation that HIV continues to wreak in under-developed countries where these new therapies are too expensive to be widely used.

For most people away from the front line, the Aids horror is over. HIV infection is containable these days, isn't it? We can stop worrying about it, right?

Wrong.

HIV has not gone away. It continues to infect gay people at an alarming rate, and although the application of these new drugs regimes seems to hold the development of the virus in check, there is no guarantee that they will remain effective for ever or that they will work for everyone. Severe side-effects also render them unsuitable for some people.

That said, and accepting that we must not become complacent, we should not underestimate what has happened in the developed world. People who are infected with HIV, and who would otherwise have succumbed to the syndrome associated with it, have been given a new lease of life. People on the verge of death have suddenly been revived by the use of these combination therapies and have gone on to live normal, productive lives. The regime of drug-taking is exacting and difficult, and not without its own perils, but only a few brief years ago, few would have anticipated that this therapy would have given a second chance to so many. For increasing numbers of people, Aids has become a manageable illness.

Describing his own experience in *Gay Times*, Michael Carter wrote: "HIV used to be about certainties. I was fairly sure when I received my HIV diagnosis in 1991 that I would live for about ten more years; I was more or less convinced that the limited arsenal of anti-HIV drugs (consisting solely of AZT with its attendant side-effects) would offer little protection against the progression of the virus."

He told of the repeated illnesses he suffered: pneumonia, TB, skin cancer. Michael had come to terms with the fact that this was likely to be the pattern of his future—one illness after another and then a premature death. But suddenly came the breakthrough. Scientists had come up with a combination of drugs that attacked HIV from several angles at once, disabling it and preventing its replication.

Initially Michael Carter was sceptical. "There had been so many reports of promising breakthroughs. But this time it proved to be different. A combination of two or three anti-HIV drugs was being proven to suppress HIV replication in the blood, boost the immune system, stop disease progression and significantly prolong life."

He eagerly participated in clinical trials in order to get early access to the new drugs. "Within weeks the blood levels of my virus were undetectable, my immune system measured in CD4 (or T-Cell) count had increased from a very low 196 to over 600 and, importantly, this translated into vastly improved physical health. No longer was I at risk of developing a life-threatening illness; the purple KS [skin cancer] patches cleared; the residual TB in my right lung was finally suppressed, and the irritating illnesses that had plagued my everyday life disappeared."

This has been the experience of many others who had assumed that their positive diagnosis was a death sentence. The cocktail of three drugs contains at least one from a class of agents known as protease inhibitors, which work by stopping the virus infecting new cells. Since the launch of protease inhibitors in 1996, many HIV-positive people have been living in better health than ever before. However, there are well-documented drawbacks to triple therapy. For some reason, the virus is able to hide out in some cells unaffected by the drugs, ready to break out as soon as therapy is stopped. The therapy itself is complicated to take—often dozens of pills are required each day, according to a complex schedule which some patients find hard to stick to.

Also, there are side effects, most notably strange redistribution of fat around the body, producing paunches, humps and other distortions.

However, new generations of all three drugs used in triple therapy are being developed which could prove better than existing agents, with fewer side effects and an easier daily dosing schedule. Researchers are also looking into the potential benefits of taking two protease inhibitors or 'dual PI therapy', as a much simpler treatment regimen which appears to be at least as effective as triple therapy.

But although there is new hope for those already infected, those who are not must keep up their guard. The education efforts must remain unrelenting, but be targeted efficiently. The safer sex message must reach the right ears. As most new cases of HIV infection still occur among gay men—at least in Western nations—it is essential that vital information is disseminated more thoroughly throughout our community. It should be aimed not only in the obvious places (such as pubs, clubs and the gay media) but in the cruising grounds and meeting places of those gay, bisexual and straight men who seek sex with other men in secret.

Some reactionary straight journalists have argued that money spent on Aids awareness is wasted because gay men "bring it on themselves" by choosing to have unsafe sex. But the world is not as simple as raving right-wing commentators and politicians would like to believe. Human needs and emotions don't always progress along a logical path and all our best intentions about safer sex can be undermined by a spur of the moment decision. The health of homosexual people is as important as that of anyone else, and we must reject spurious arguments about the money being better spent on more common illnesses.

Difficult though it is, we must continue our efforts to integrate safer sex into our lives at all times. It isn't easy, and there is growing evidence that younger people are reluctant to heed the safer sex message, but despite the lapses, we must go on trying.

What is Aids?

Acquired Immune Deficiency Syndrome is caused by the Human Immunodeficiency Virus (HIV). A syndrome is a collection of symptoms which, when taken together, indicate a particular condition. Once HIV is present in the body it can severely compromise the working of our complicated immune system. When these natural defences are down, the sufferer is open to attack from a number of otherwise rare diseases, like the skin cancer Kaposi's Sarcoma and "opportunistic infections", such as pneumonia and toxoplasmosis. In normal circumstances the body is highly effective in repelling these infections and infestations, but when the immune system has been severely damaged there is little power of resistance and the infections and malignancies eventually overcome and kill the sufferer. Although each individual opportunistic infection can be treated, usually another disease comes along to replace it, gradually wearing down the victim.

It is important to understand the difference between HIV infection and Aids. If someone is HIV positive it simply means that a test has revealed that he has antibodies to the virus in his bloodstream. When HIV enters the bloodstream it can take from six weeks to three months before the antibodies appear. In some people the delay can be as much as six months. The virus can then lay dormant in the body for many years before there is any other indication of infection. During that period, the infected person can be perfectly healthy and functioning in a normal way. It is only when the virus starts to multiply and attack the immune system that the sufferer begins to experience the infections and illnesses that indicate Aids.

How is HIV spread?

HIV is primarily a blood-borne virus, but it has been found in varying concentrations in other bodily fluids such as semen and saliva. This means that not all bodily fluids are equally infectious.

Most HIV infections are sexually acquired, although the virus has also been spreading among drug users who share dirty needles. A significant number of haemophiliacs were affected by HIV before it was realised that the blood products used in their treatment had been contaminated by the virus. All blood products in Britain and the US are now screened and treated to ensure that HIV is removed.

HIV does not spread through casual social contact—it is an infection not a contagion. It does not spread through shaking someone's hand, sneezing or using the same toilet as someone who is infected. If it were so easily spread, say by coughing, there would be millions more cases than there are already, and the incidence of cases would be much wider. HIV cannot live in swimming pools, on lavatory seats or damp towels. Although they suck blood, mosquitoes cannot transmit HIV, nor can bed bugs, lice, fleas or ticks. You cannot acquire HIV from donating blood and, in industrialised countries, all donated blood is now tested for HIV infection before it is used.

HIV is very fragile once it is outside the body and dies off quickly when it comes into contact with air. No health worker dealing with people with Aids has been known to acquire the virus except through accidental needle-stick injuries or failure to follow simple precautions such as covering cuts before dealing with patients who were bleeding. No family of a person with Aids (discounting sexual partners) is known to have been infected with HIV, even though they have nursed their relatives through the terminal stages of their illness. Mothers and fathers and brothers and sisters have continued to kiss and cuddle their family member through the period when nursing was required and there are no proven cases of them developing Aids or becoming infected with HIV. A few simple hygiene measures are sufficient to protect those who care for people with Aids:

- Spilt blood and other bodily fluids should be cleaned up with household bleach diluted one part in ten with water. Gloves should be worn.
- Blood and other bodily fluids in contact with the skin should be washed off with soap and water. Bleach should not be used on the skin.
- Cuts, scratches and other abrasions on the skin should be covered with a waterproof dressing until a scab forms.
- Be careful with sharp objects that could carry blood or other bodily fluids—such as razors and hypodermic needles—in case these accidentally puncture the skin.
- Clothing and sheets, including those soiled with blood or other bodily fluids, should be washed in a machine at a high temperature setting. Gloves should be worn when handling soiled items.
- Razors and toothbrushes should not be shared.
- Crockery and cutlery should be washed in hot water with a detergent.

These are the usual precautions which need to be taken with any infectious disease.

Much of the hysteria which has surrounded Aids has been created by misleading newspaper stories. Fortunately, much of this irrational fear has now subsided, and there are very few people who still believe that they can catch HIV from eating food which has been cooked by gay chefs or from beer glasses or any of the other foolish things that were of concern at the beginning of the crisis. Indeed, it is much more likely that a person with Aids would be at risk from associating with "healthy" people, because of his weakened immunity, he is much more likely to catch something from them than they are from him.

If you have, in fact, already acquired HIV, you will have discovered by now that there is a wide range of support available to you. This has been created in the main by gay people themselves, and you should make full use of it. Many people living with HIV have come to realise, after the shock and depression have worn off, that the situation is far from being hopeless. With the help of these new drugs, they may be able to go on and live a normal life span. However, the effectiveness of these new drugs in apparently reducing the virus in the bloodstream to undetectable levels should not give the impression that you are no longer infectious. New research seems to suggest that semen can remain highly infected with different types of HIV while the virus may not be detectable in blood. Scientists in the USA and Switzerland have found a variant of HIV in the genital tract. This means that a patient whose levels of HIV in his blood have been drastically reduced by drug treatment, may still have high concentrations of the disease-causing agent in his semen. A study of 44 HIV-positive men in North Carolina and Switzerland found that anti-Aids drugs had different effects on the viruses depending on where they were situated. The implications of this are clear— you cannot assume that you are non-infectious simply because the virus seems to have disappeared from your blood stream after starting a combination therapy regime.

At the time of writing, Aids is still not curable, although for many people it has become containable and manageable.

There is no vaccine which will prevent infection, and maybe there never will be, although scientists continue their search. The only real preventative against infection is an awareness of how the virus is transmitted, accompanied by a determination that it will not get into your body.

Should I be tested for HIV?

Because HIV is present in the bloodstream, one way of detecting it is through a blood sample. At present it is difficult to detect the live virus so the test is for antibodies to HIV. Antibodies are made by your body's immune system when it meets a virus or other invasive organism. Some antibodies destroy invading viruses. Others, like those produced when HIV enters the bloodstream, do not protect you. They act as a signal that you have been infected at some point. The HIV test cannot tell you how long ago the infection took place. If you take the test and it shows you are antibody positive it probably means you will be infectious for the rest of your life. Because of the delay that can occur between infection and the appearance of the antibodies, some clinics will ask you to return after six months for another test if the first one was negative.

It is difficult to know just how many people who have been infected with the virus will go on to develop the full-scale syndrome. It is not properly understood what influence other factors might have on the likelihood of Aids developing. It has been suggested that the likelihood of infection is increased by drug abuse, malnutrition and previous infections, especially with other strains of HIV or STDs (such as syphilis). The affected person's genetic make up and their emotional state may also be relevant.

So, how do you know if you have been at risk of infection? These are the most common ways that the virus passes from one person to another:

• Penetrative intercourse without a condom. Anal sex is the most efficient way for the virus to pass from one person to another, although, as we've said, it can also pass through vaginal sex. It is still not entirely clear how risky giving or getting oral sex is. There does seem to be evidence that the virus can pass in this way more easily than previously thought. Other

sexually transmitted diseases can infect the mouth
and throat through oral sex.
- Sharing needles or injecting equipment (including
tattoo needles). If you are injecting drugs you should
use new equipment every time. Tattooists should
always sterilise their equipment.

If you haven't done either of these things, and you haven't
had a blood transfusion in a third world country, then the
chances are very slim that you have HIV.

If you feel you may have been at risk, not knowing your
status might be very stressful. It also means that you cannot
begin a course of therapy which might spare you much of the
pain and discomfort that goes with this disease.

In the end, each gay man who suspects he might be infected
has to decide for himself whether or not he takes the test. By
going to the right place—a sexually transmitted disease clinic
rather than your GP—you will be properly counselled by
health advisors who know all about the consequences of
having the test, taking into account your own particular
circumstances. Make full use of these counsellors. If you
decide to go ahead, you will see a doctor who will tell you
what the test involves and may ask you about your sexual
history over the past six months or so. You will have to give a
sample of blood which will undergo several tests to be sure
that the result is correct.

What the result means
A negative result can mean that you are not infected or that
you haven't yet developed the antibodies to HIV. To be
absolutely certain, you may have to return after six months
for another test to confirm the original. Naturally, after being
given a negative result, many men will run laughing from the
clinic and want to celebrate. Don't celebrate with unsafe sex
or drugs.

However well you may have prepared yourself for it, a positive result will still come as a profound shock. You may feel resigned and helpless, having strongly suspected that this would happen, or you may be despairing, confused and deeply depressed. You will be offered support by the health advisor. He or she will give you information about agencies that can help you come to terms with what has happened and to accept and adjust to your status. The doctor may ask you to tell him who you have had unprotected sex within the past three months. He may want to contact these people to tell them that they may be at risk, or he may ask you to do it. You don't have to give this information if you don't want to, but it would be the responsible thing to do.

Allow yourself plenty of time before deciding whom you tell about your status. Although people may promise to keep your secret, sometimes they won't, and that could be catastrophic. There is no need for your work colleagues to know what your result is—or even that you are having the test. Some gay men have already found to their cost that normally level-headed colleagues have become completely irrational when faced with this issue.

If you want to seek support from your family, there might be the double problem of coming out about your sexuality as well as your HIV status. This is a lot of devastating information for them to take in at one go, and you might want to enlist professional help to get you all through it.

Professional counsellors who will be at your disposal can be a magnificent asset which you should make full use of. Talking to them is not a sign that you can't cope or that you are weak—on the contrary, it will be one of the most constructive steps you can take in the difficult process of coming to terms with your diagnosis.

The test result you have had will not tell you what the implications are for your health. Nor can it tell you how long you have been infected.

If you do not wish your GP to be told of the result, ensure that you agree this with the clinic beforehand—your GP cannot guarantee the same level of confidentiality that an

STD clinic can. However, you will need to think carefully about this issue, because your GP's help could be very important if you are given a positive diagnosis. If you are sent to other departments within the hospital, the specialist there will probably be told your result, this is then likely to go into your general hospital notes which tend to be less confidential than those in the STD clinic. Who knows who might see your result? It will, of course, be appropriate for a few people to know so that they can take the necessary precautions. To reduce the risk of unnecessary disclosure, confide in a senior member of staff—a doctor or charge nurse—and ask them to ensure that your records are kept secure. In hospitals outside the big cities, it is still quite rare to see cases of Aids or HIV infection, and there might still be some crude prejudice among the staff in such places. In units specialising in the treatment of Aids, it is unlikely that any of these problems will arise.

In 1994 the Association of British Insurers announced that they would change the controversial question about HIV antibody tests on their application forms from "Have you ever had an HIV test" to "Have you ever had a positive HIV test". This they said would be fairer all round, as previously many people who had behaved responsibly and had a test which had proved negative were being penalised. The ABI says that anyone who had been refused cover as the result of an earlier response would still be rejected. However, "lifestyle" questionnaires will still be sent to applicants. As *The Financial Time*s pointed out: "Even when insurers produce new forms which drop the question about Aids-testing, they will still be able to find out whether you have had an Aids test from your GP's medical records." If you refuse them permission to contact your GP, they will simply turn down your application. Your chances of getting a mortgage, too, might also be affected if it becomes known that you have been tested for HIV, whatever the result. You should be aware of the Access to Medical Reports Act, 1988, which gives you some rights to see medical reports before they are issued.

Insurers would also be likely to demand that anyone seeking a large amount of life cover would require an HIV test.

Whether you are positive, negative or don't know, you must practise safer sex. Even if you are on combination therapies and your tests are telling you that the virus has fallen to undetectable levels in your blood stream, you must continue to practise safer sex. This will not only protect those who are not infected, but also those who are HIV positive and who must not risk acquiring further infections which might increase their chances of becoming ill.

Many of the support and advice groups which have been established in the Aids field can offer expert counselling and much experience. They will have up to date information about treatment options, diet, social security implications and other important considerations. You will find some of them listed in the back of this book. Before you rush into a decision, spend some time exploring all the issues.

I'm positive—should I be on combination therapy?

If you are thinking of starting anti-HIV therapy, make sure you know which drugs are the most suitable to take for your own situation. Not all anti-HIV treatments are the same. With some, the dosing schedule is easier than with others, and it is widely recognised that drugs with simpler dosing may help you adhere to your treatment regimen. Choosing your treatment and making a commitment to taking it properly means you are giving yourself the best chance of staying well and symptom free.

Many doctors now believe that the best chance of delaying the progress of HIV infection is to hit the virus hard when starting treatment. To do this, triple therapy with anti-HIV drugs is now being used by many doctors as soon as this decision has been made. This approach has been shown to be highly effective in suppressing the virus and helps prevent

HIV becoming resistant. In turn, this may improve your chance of living a symptom-free life.

Only you and your doctor can decide if and when to begin taking anti-HIV drugs. When the decision is made to start, you want the maximum chance of success. That means taking your tablets every day, at the right dose, at the right time and in the right way. If you stop, reduce or miss a dose, it may allow the virus to become resistant—resistance can make your therapy much less effective.

If you find you are missing doses, or becoming confused about what you've taken, do discuss it with your doctor. It may be possible to tailor your medication schedule to suit your lifestyle. Or you might be able to discuss changing your treatment, perhaps to a combination with fewer tablets to take each day.

There are some simple things you can do to help yourself. For example:

- divide your tablets into daily doses at the beginning of each week
- tie in taking your tablets with other things you do regularly. Some people find a good visual prompt is to keep the tablets where they can see them.
- check whether tablets need to be taken before, with, or after food.
- take care when your routine changes, for instance at weekends or on holiday.

Research shows that the commonest reason for the failure of these combination treatments is their complexity. It can be very hard to remember which tablets must be taken when, especially when you break your routine, as when you go on holiday. It takes commitment and concentration to get it right, but it is worth the effort. Hopefully new drugs that are less demanding will soon be developed.

The future

Already thousands of our number are HIV positive. Many of our dearest friends died before these new drug breakthroughs became available. Despite the new optimism, there is no guarantee that these new regimes will remain effective over the long term. HIV is a smart bug, and has the capacity to mutate frequently to outwit such onslaughts. We hope fervently that this will not happen, but no-one can be certain. The nightmare may start again, and our commitment to safer sex and to our own health must remain undimmed. There are signs that gay men are becoming bored with what many see as unreasonable restrictions on their lives. A new generation that has not been subjected to the horrors of premature death on a large scale is emerging, and we must try hard to ensure that they do not have to learn the lesson again, the hard way.

Prejudice, ignorance and homophobia still dictate much of what happens in relation to Aids. Right-wing pressure groups and religious organisations have tried to hijack the syndrome as a campaigning tool. They have succeeded in blocking many initiatives that might have proved useful, some try to obstruct further spending on the disease, and they devalue the lives of gay people in the process. Education initiatives come under constant attack in the pages of the tabloid press, being presented as "an obscene waste of money" and a scandal. But there is no way that we can successfully confront a sexually transmitted disease without being honest about sex.

There is a great battle to be fought against these forces of hatred, and gay people have risen to the challenge. Aids has brought many people out of the closet who would otherwise not have made the journey.

The most effective steps in the fields of education, support and fund raising have been taken by the gay communities themselves. We all have a part to play in this, whether by donating money, becoming actively involved in the Aids support and education network, or simply by living our lives as gay men with dignity and honour. We can fight back against those who try to use Aids as a political weapon.

Fortunately, we now know enough about HIV to avoid being infected by it. An awareness of how the virus is transmitted and what steps we can take to keep it out of our bodies is knowledge that has been gained at the cost of many lives. At present, safer sex is our only weapon, and we must use it sensibly and constantly.

Other health concerns

Aids has dominated our thinking so much over the past decade that other sexually transmitted diseases have been relegated to a much less important status. And, naturally, any steps we take to protect ourselves against Aids will have the knock-on effect of protecting us against many of these other diseases. However, we should still be aware of what further perils might befall the sexually active gay man.

Syphilis

Syphilis is one of the most dangerous venereal diseases and because the symptoms vary so widely between patients, it is not always recognised. In its final stages it can produce devastating effects and can ultimately kill.

The disease is generally, but not always, passed on by sexual contact. You can't catch it from a toilet seat, door handle or teacup—the bacteria can only survive for a few moments away from the warm, moist human environment which they favour.

The bacterium *Treponema pallidum* thrives in the genitals, but can inhabit the mouth, anus or tonsils during the primary stages. The syphilis bacterium can pass from one person to another with even the most transitory touch: it doesn't need prolonged contact. Occasionally it enters the body through a dry surface, like the finger, if there is a small scratch or cut to provide a doorway.

The first sign of syphilis is the appearance of a sore or chancre: it is about the size of a pea and usually shows itself about three or four weeks after the infection occurs. But it could be as little as ten days or as long as three months before it appears. The bacteria may have entered the body in a concealed place—the rectum or inside the mouth, for instance. There, the chancre might not be noticed. In some cases there is a painless swelling of the glands in the area of the chancre.

If you don't spot the disease at this point, the chancre will disappear within one to eight weeks and you will enter the second stage. A rash will appear, maybe on the chest, the back, the legs or the arms—or even on the soles of the feet or the palms of the hands, which aren't usually prone to rashes. The rash varies from person to person. In some it is noticeable with lumps and bumps of various sizes; in others it will go unnoticed with, perhaps, just a few pimples on the shoulder. There could be a mild fever, a general feeling of tiredness or even some hair loss. Then again, none of these symptoms need necessarily occur. Such is the unpredictable and treacherous nature of syphilis.

Over the whole of this period, the patient will be highly infectious.

Within two weeks, the secondary stage will be over and the *Treponema* will go into hiding. All seems well. There are no further symptoms and for some victims there will be no further signs of the disease (even though the bacteria remains within the body). For others, after a period of time— sometimes decades—the disease reappears for the third or tertiary stage. It may attack the heart or the nervous system, severely disabling or killing the victim.

If caught in the early stages however, treatment with penicillin or some other antibiotic will rapidly and completely cure syphilis.

If you have any suspicion that you might have contracted syphilis, contact your special clinic or doctor without delay.

Gonorrhoea
Also known as clap or a dose, it is one of the most common of the venereal diseases. Although it isn't as dangerous as syphilis, under no circumstances should it be left untreated.

Once again, the mode of transmission is by close contact. However, gonorrhoea isn't just a disease of the sex organs, but of the mucous membranes and can occur in the urethral passage of the penis (the tube down which semen and urine pass), in the rectum, the eyes, the mouth or the throat.

Perhaps the first indication of a gonorrhoeal infection is a discharge of thick, yellow pus from the penis. It might become obvious at first on the pyjamas or underpants. There might be a burning sensation when urinating. If it's in the throat it will produce symptoms rather like those of the common cold; if in the eyes there will be tears, irritation and pus. If it has been contracted anally there will be soreness and a constant urge to defecate. Bowel movements might be preceded by a spurt of yellow pus.

Occasionally there are no symptoms at all and you might not be aware that you have been infected. If left untreated, however, gonorrhoea can lead to a form of arthritis which particularly affects the knees, elbows, ankles and wrists. If the eyes are infected, blindness can follow. If you are at risk, a regular check is the answer.

Treatment is simple and effective. A course of penicillin (or other antibiotic) will generally do the job. Obviously you should refrain from sex while you are infected and keep your hands scrupulously clean, especially if you wear contact lenses.

Crabs

The *Phthirus pubis* or crab louse thrives in the pubic area, but can make a home in any hairy part of the body. It's called a crab louse because under the microscope that's exactly what it looks like. To the naked eye it is the size of a pinhead. You'll know crabs are around when you start to itch, and close inspection might reveal them crawling about. They are most visible when they have just fed (on the victim's blood) and the bites they inflict can lead to localised soreness. Being infected with crabs is more of a nuisance than a danger, but it is advisable to rid yourself of them as soon as possible.

Crabs are generally passed on by bodily contact, but they can survive away from their human hosts for up to twenty-four hours. This is one pest you *can* pick up from a toilet seat or infested bedding.

There are simple self-treatments which you can buy from the chemist without prescription—Carylderm, Quellada, Derbac M or Prioderm. Some crabs have developed a resistance to some of the insecticide shampoos, so you may have to try more than one brand. It is important that you follow the instructions on the packet to the letter.

Don't be tempted to squirt yourself with fly sprays and the like—the results of doing this can be far worse than having crabs in the first place. After treatment, clothes must be given a very hot wash to ensure all the lice and eggs are destroyed; this also applies to bedding, dressing gowns, pyjamas and so on. Cloth-covered furniture and carpets where the lice might be lurking should also be cleaned.

NSU

Non-specific urethritis (NSU) bears a superficial resemblance to gonorrhoea. It is a little understood but very common STD and can be difficult to eradicate. It seems to be able to lie dormant and flare up again from time to time. While not apparently dangerous, NSU can be painful and should be properly treated.

Hepatitis

Hepatitis is a serious viral infection of the liver. There are three main viruses involved, the hepatitis A virus (HAV) hepatitis B virus (HBV) and the relatively recently discovered Hepatitis C virus (HCV).

Hepatitis A is an unpleasant illnesses and the patient is usually jaundiced (that is to say, his skin turns yellow). However, there are generally no long-term effects and in time the patient usually recovers. The hepatitis A virus is predominantly contracted through infected food and water.

Hepatitis C is another nasty version, and because it has

only recently been identified, less is known about it. However, it appears to be an insidious organism which attacks the liver. It enters the liver cells and multiplies, forcing the body's immune system to destroy the infected cells. It may take a long time—thirty or forty years, perhaps—but it can eventually completely destroy the liver. Cirrhosis develops in 20-40 per cent of carriers, some others may develop liver cancer. There is no proven treatment for infection with HCV at the moment, although research is forging ahead. It isn't clear how the virus is transmitted, but research seems to indicate that sharing dirty needles is one route. So far there is no evidence to show that it is particularly related to the gay lifestyle.

Hepatitis B, however, is very much a disease prevalent among gay men, and is a very serious infection. It spreads most effectively through sexual activity. The virus is blood-borne, like HIV, and is transmitted in much the same way. Past studies have indicated that up to 50% of the gay men tested showed themselves to have antibodies to the hepatitis B virus, indicating infection at some time in the past.

Since Aids made its appearance, and many gay men began to practise safer sex, the incidence of hepatitis B has begun to diminish. However, there is no room for complacency; the number of reported cases still runs into tens of thousands and hepatitis B has been described as a hundred times more infectious than HIV.

Initial symptoms may appear between four and twenty-six weeks after contact with the hepatitis B virus. They include tiredness, nausea, lack of appetite and aversion to alcohol and smoking. The acute stage of the illness may also include jaundice, fever, dark urine, pale stools and abdominal tenderness in the area of the liver, which is also often enlarged. After this stage there follows a prolonged convalescence of up to six months when the sufferer will be lethargic and depressed.

However, in 50% of the cases there may be no symptoms at all or they may be so insignificant as to go unrecognised or be mistaken for mild flu. During the illness the hepatitis B virus can be detected in the blood by looking for the whole virus. The virus may disappear from the blood after about six months, but in about 10% of cases a high level of virus is retained beyond this period and this indicates that the sufferer has become a carrier—even though outwardly he appears healthy. The level of infectiousness varies between one carrier and another.

There is no cure available for hepatitis B once it has been contracted, although the majority of people affected make a full if slow recovery. Some, however, do not survive.

The good news is that a very effective vaccine (developed with the help of hundreds of gay men in New York) is now available. If you are sexually active, you should give serious consideration to having this vaccination. It offers over 90% protection against the disease over five years, after a course of three injections over six months. Although the vaccine is made from blood products, it has been specially treated so that there is no risk of your contracting HIV from it.

In Britain the vaccine is available on the National Health Service to those who are deemed to be at risk. However, provision of the vaccine is at the discretion of the doctor, and not all of them are willing to prescribe it on demand. If you cannot persuade him/her to give you the vaccine, then you might consider paying for it privately. The price is cheap compared to what a bout of hepatitis B might cost.

Herpes

Herpes simplex can appear almost anywhere on the body, but it can be spread through sexual contact and so is often found on the penis and anus. The symptoms are blisters which can be intensely painful before they burst and begin to heal—after which the symptoms disappear. The virus, however, remains dormant in the body awaiting the opportunity to resurface, generally when the sufferer is run down or depressed.

Herpes is infectious while the blisters are present, but there are creams that can reduce the pain and some people have benefited from homeopathic treatment. It should be noted that herpes can be a devastating infection in pregnant women because of the damage the virus can cause the baby.

Oral sex is out when you have cold sores on your lips, too.

Precautions

There are more than twenty other diseases and infestations which can be loosely termed sexually transmitted and you should make it your business to learn about them. Get a good handbook on the subject and keep it on your shelf for reference. Such is the ignorance about STDs that many people wouldn't know if they had one or, if they did, would be unaware of the potentially grave consequences of leaving it untreated. Those who neglect these infections while continuing to have sex are irresponsible in the extreme.

If you are not part of a monogamous couple, but are sexually active, try to get regular check-ups at the local STD clinic, (called GUM or special clinics in some areas). These are usually attached to general hospitals and you'll find them listed under "Venereal Diseases" in the local phone book. Alternatively, ring the hospital switchboard and ask for the number. There will be no moralising when you go to the clinic for treatment; the health workers have seen it all before and their only concern is to prevent the further spread of these nasty ailments. They will ask you to trace and inform your recent partner(s). Discretion is the byword at Special Clinics and you will be issued with a number to ensure anonymity. You should be prepared for an examination of your genitals and for possible follow-up treatment.

Obviously hygiene and cleanliness are a starting point in protecting yourself. However, some of the viruses and bacteria are extremely hardy and can survive even the most scrupulous washing. Taking a shower before and after sex is always a good idea, though. As with HIV, your best friend is a condom—treasure that friendship and make the best use of it.

Testicular Cancer

Testicular cancer is the most common form of cancer in young men in the UK and it occurs mostly between the ages of 19 and 44. It is easily treatable if caught early—and is curable in 99% of cases. The first sign is usually a swelling in one of the testicles or a pea sized lump on the front or side of one of your balls. There may be a dull ache, but there is seldom pain.

In order to catch the disease before it has the chance to spread, it is essential that you check your balls at least once a month. Regular checking will make you familiar with what your testicles feel like and therefore it will be easier for you to know if there are any changes. Try to do your self-examination after a bath or shower when the balls are hanging loose.

Only three per cent of young men regularly check their testicles—mostly because they just don't know how to do it. So here are the simple instructions for this important self-examination.

- Stand in front of a mirror and look for any swelling on the skin of the scrotum. One testicle may appear larger than the other and one may hang lower, which is not unusual.
- Hold each testicle gently between the thumb and fingertips of both hands and slowly bring the thumb and fingertips of one hand together while relaxing the fingertips of the other.
- Alternate this several times so that the testicle glides smoothly between both sets of fingers. This allows you to assess the shape and texture of the testis.
- You mustn't press too hard and you must be careful not to twist the testicle.
- Each testicle should feel soft and smooth, like a hard boiled egg without its shell.

Any lump, swelling, irregularity, abnormal hardness, tenderness or any change within the body of the testicle itself should be reported to your doctor. Testicular cancer almost always occurs in only one testicle.

There are reasons other than cancer why testicles might be swollen, so don't jump to any conclusion. Some of these are:

1. A Hydrocoele. This is a soft painless cyst. During development, the membrane lining of the abdomen pouches down into the scrotum as the testicles descend. This closes off to leave an empty remnant in the scrotum. In middle age this remnant often fills with fluid and can grow quite large. In most cases there is no underlying cause, but occasionally a hydrocoele forms as a result of inflammation, infection or injury or—rarely—an underlying tumour of the testicle on that side.

2. Epididymal cyst. This is a harmless swelling arising from the epididymis, the coiled collection of tubes attached to the back of the testes. Small pea-sized epididymal cysts are common in men over 40. These cysts are filled with colourless fluid and are usually left in place rather than removed.

3. A varicocele. This is a collection of varicose veins surrounding the testicle and is one of the commonest reasons for an enlarged testicle. There may be aching and discomfort, although it is harmless. Any discomfort can be relieved by wearing an athletic support or tight underpants.

More than 50 per cent of sufferers from testicular cancer don't go to their doctor until after the cancer has started to spread. This makes it more difficult and sometimes impossible to treat successfully and its side-effects become more unpleasant.

Testicular cancer is still quite rare, with just over 1,500 new cases a year in the UK. It is not known what causes it, but men who were born with an undescended or partly descended testicle are five times more likely to develop testicular cancer. Other research has suggested that there may be a hereditary factor involved, and that if you have a father or brother who has developed testicular cancer you are at increased risk.

A brother with testicular cancer means that you can be ten times more likely to develop it. Treatment for testicular cancer shouldn't affect your sex life in the long term.

Prostate problems

For older men—over forty-five—there is a distinct possibility of problems with the prostate. This chestnut-shaped internal gland, situated just below the bladder, plays a part in the manufacture of semen. As we grow older the prostate begins to swell. Because it surrounds the urethral tube—down which we pee—it can cause a constriction and subsequently problems with urination. If you find that you are having problems with your waterworks—slow to get started, then stopping and starting or dribbling after you've finished, getting up more than three times a night to go to the loo— consult your GP who will be able to help you out with the problem. Don't be embarrassed. The majority of men will encounter problems with the prostate as they begin to age, so your doctor will be well experienced at spotting problems.

Relationship with your doctor

If you go to your doctor with a STD it is important that you tell him or her all the relevant facts. You may be reluctant to go to your GP—especially if the site of the infection is the rectal area—because you are afraid of a bad reaction. Remember you can visit a STD clinic without an appointment and your doctor need never know. If, however, you do decide to seek treatment from your GP, and he/she proves judgmental, you should get yourself another doctor as soon as possible, ensuring that the new doctor doesn't have the same attitudes as the old one. In Britain you can transfer from one family doctor to another without having to give a reason—

contact your local Family Practitioner Committee (number in the phone book) for information about how to do this. Similarly, doctors can remove you from their list if they regard you as a nuisance—or for other reasons. In these days of tight budgetary controls it is often difficult to know the real reasons why some 90,000 people are removed from GPs lists in Britain each year.

Prevention is better than cure...

...especially if there is no cure, as with Aids. As well as trying hard to be aware of the dangers of STDs, many gay men are looking towards improving their general health through exercise, better diet and watching their intake of alcohol, cigarettes and other drugs. This is all-important for the maintenance of health and fitness. And a healthy body goes a long way toward a healthy mind. It's much more difficult to be a happy homosexual if you're a poorly one.

Regular and sufficient sleep is important, as is a quiet and relaxed mind. Many gay events, like discos, go on until the early hours and they inevitably take their toll if indulged in to excess. Enjoy yourself, by all means, but make sure that you aren't burning the candle at both ends too often.

If you're living alone it is important that you pay special attention to your diet. Try not to fall into the habit of only eating easily-prepared junk food. Not only will it make you fat, it will, if eaten at the expense of a more balanced diet, lower your resistance to illness. Junk food is fine for the occasional indulgence but not as a staple diet. There are many excellent cooking-for-one recipe books crammed with tasty ideas, with tips on effective storage and economical shopping for small quantities. You don't have to be a great chef to prepare acceptable, tasty and balanced meals. Get interested in a bigger variety of foods—after all, eating is not only an essential element of life, it can also be one of its great pleasures; try to savour it. Make efforts to overcome any prejudices you might have against vegetarianism, ethnic cooking or low-fat foods. With a bit of thought and practice, you could be making a valuable investment for the future. And if you can't bring yourself to make a lot of effort just to cook for one, then occasionally invite friends over for a meal, and that will give you the impetus to try new dishes and cooking techniques. Don't depend entirely on the frying pan.

So, for a healthier gay lifestyle:

- Avoid risky sex activities. Make condoms a familiar part of your life.
- Whenever you are thinking of having sex with someone you don't know well, keep an eye open for these signs:
  - A chancre or sore that is a characteristic of syphilis. It might be on the penis, anus, lips or mouth.
  - Skin rashes, especially around the anus or lips.
  - A discharge of pus at the opening of the penis.
  - Herpes blisters. If cold sores are present you should avoid oral sex.
  - Swollen glands anywhere in the body. But remember, often there are no visible signs of HIV infection or other STDs.
- If you think you have any symptoms of a sexually transmitted disease, stop all sexual activity with others and seek medical attention immediately.
- Eat properly. A good diet should include balanced amounts of the following food groups: dairy products; fruit and vegetables; meat (including fish and poultry); carbohydrates (bread and cereals, pasta, rice, potatoes). If you're eating vegetarian, ensure you understand how to achieve a balance so that you get all the nutrition you need. Include as little sugar, salt and alcohol as you can. Increase the amount of fruit and vegetables you are eating at the moment by at least fifty per cent.
- Cut down on cigarettes and booze. Everyone tells you this: there must be something in it.
- Stop using drugs for "recreational" purposes. The long-term effects, even of poppers, are unknown.

- Get sufficient sleep. The fashion for late-night entertainment can play havoc with health in the long term, especially if, by nature, you are a "daytime person".
- Regular exercise makes the body healthier, more resistant to infection as well as more attractive. Swimming or taking long walks can help. There's no need to make a lifestyle out of keeping fit, although working out at the gym is a very popular pastime among gay men, and if you're searching for gay friends, it isn't a bad place to start looking. The Gay Outdoor Club is another popular way to keep active while meeting new friends. It has groups all over the country. The contact address is at the back of this book.
- Don't underestimate the damaging effects on your ears of frequent exposure to loud music. The preponderance of discos in the gay lifestyle makes this a real problem, but one which isn't often addressed—until difficulties with hearing develop. Stand away from powerful speakers, and maybe even consider using ear-plugs for part of your evening.
- Check yourself monthly for any changes in the shape, size or weight of your testicles.

Respect your body, take care of it, and you will find that happiness will be that much easier to pursue.

8: The ethical way to happiness

"Happiness is the only good.
The place to be happy is here.
The time to be happy is now.
The way to be happy is to make others so."
- Robert G. Ingersoll.

Diversity is a word you will come across over and over again in gay life. It is used to describe the many and varied types of gay people and their equally contrasting ways of life. It indicates that there is not one "gay lifestyle" but many, and that we gay people cannot be defined in a way that suggests that there are particular characteristics that are common to us all. Our enemies then go one step further and say that because gay people don't necessarily have anything in common with each other beyond their sexual desire for members of their own gender, there cannot be a gay community. It is accepted that there are black communities (which share the same culture and gather together in the same areas) or Jewish communities (who have their religion, culture and sometimes location in common), but not gay communities. After all, it is argued, all gay people share is a desire for sex with people of the same gender.

It may be true that we don't live in ghettos, and that we don't often live in family groups like ethnic communities do (gay mother, gay father, gay children, gay neighbours? That would be something!), but we *do* share other things besides sexual desires. We are all potentially subject to the same pressures, the same discrimination and the same alienation. And so we gather together not only to socialise and meet each other for sex, but to talk about how we can make life better for gay people and challenge the prejudice that surrounds us. We create support groups, help-lines and political lobbying campaigns. All over the country, gay people are working to make things better for those fellow gays who are less fortunate than they are.

So, we have diverse communities, too, created (often locally) to fit the needs of the people who use them. These communities are frequently small and revolve around a pub or club. Sometimes they are big and influential, such as in London and Manchester. They feel connected to the national and international identity by the gay media and by larger scale events like Pride.

There are plenty of good, selfless, committed and responsible gay people in these communities. But, sadly, there are many maladjusted individuals who have been deeply damaged by their inability to shake off the feeling that they are inferior. And there is the ever-present temptation on the gay scene to live excessive and, ultimately, destructive, lifestyles.

This chapter is about how to gain some kind of balance in your life so that you do not fall into the traps that have robbed so many gay people in the past of their happiness.

Facing the facts

There is a famous line in the play *The Boys in the Band* which goes: "Show me a happy homosexual and I'll show you a gay corpse." The character who utters it is a self-loathing gay man who has convinced himself that life for gay people is inevitably a vale of tears.

The Boys in the Band was written in the nineteen sixties, when there was still a heavy overhang of oppression and self-oppression from the preceding generations. For centuries, homosexuality had been "the love that dare not speak its name", and the shame and guilt that had been heaped on gay people, and the contempt with which they were treated, was not to be erased in a few short years.

We know much more about ourselves now, and we look on *The Boys in the Band* as a museum piece, an interesting glimpse at a past era. But when speaking to young gay people, even now, it is difficult to conclude that we have solved all our problems and that we all live the life we want, free from doubts about our value. The deep loathing that the characters in *The Boys in the Band* felt for themselves, and each other, is still around in the gay community, although tempered by an undoubted relaxing of public disapproval.

Now our detractors in the straight community, and some in the gay community, have taken a new tack. Having accepted that there are gay communities, they have begun to criticise the way many gay people treat each other and the unhealthy way that our communities have developed. (For an example of this, see the book *Anti-Gay* published by Cassell and edited by Mark Simpson).

Our critics say that we are wildly promiscuous and sex-crazed, that we are immature, irresponsible, and self-obsessed. They say that the community we have created is a youth and beauty oriented nightmare from which the unattractive and the old are casually debarred. We are cruel and rejecting of those who do not have perfect bodies or pretty or handsome faces. They say we are manipulated into uniformity by commercial forces—we all have to look the same, drink the same beer, have the same haircut, go to the same bars and are slaves to fads and fashions. They say that any criticism of our behaviour—however justifiable it might be—is immediately dismissed as homophobia.

They say we are immoral.

Most gay people will bridle when they read this list of charges, and immediately become defensive. This is not a description of *my* life, they protest. But the time has come for us to drop the defensiveness, and to step back and take an objective look at what our critics say. Is there any truth in the accusations they level at us?

Naturally, all generalisations will be unfair. As we have discovered in previous chapters, stereotypes—by which whole groups of people are portrayed as sharing the same characteristics and personality traits—are dangerous and misleading; but in every cliché there lurks an element of truth. The question is: how much of what our critics say is true? The time has come to be painfully honest with ourselves as we attempt to come up with an answer.

In many respects, the gay community is much more sophisticated now than it ever has been in the past, and we are mature enough as a group to be able to face up to the fact that not everything in the gay garden is rosy. There is room for the kind of improvement that will benefit us all.

I realise that it is dangerous to write about the failings of others without admitting to one's own failures, and so I will put my hand up now and say that I have led a far from blameless life. But I have learned a few lessons on the way, and I have thought carefully about the mistakes I have made. I am not here to lay on a guilt trip, because I am as guilty as anyone else of the behaviours I am about to discuss.

In an earlier chapter I wrote that we should question everything that is said about us, and that in the end we must make our own way in life, often in the face of strong resistance from those who are important to us. I have counselled you to think carefully about religious objections to your sexuality and to reject superstitious calls to become a sexless, lonely robot. I urged you to think for yourself and not to order your life to please others. But there comes a time when the rejection of other people's opinions has to be judged against what is ethically acceptable. Making up rules that fit our circumstances—which are often radically different from the circumstances of the average heterosexual—does not mean that we should just behave in any way we wish, free from any moral code.

Many of the charges that are made about the behaviour of gay people can also be made about heterosexuals, but in this book we are looking at our own community and the way we live within it. Often on the gay scene you will see people whose behaviour is aimed entirely at self-gratification. They, like every other gay person, have had to reassess their approach to life in the light of their sexuality, but they have, in the process, thrown out the ethical baby with the bath water. There is a difference between saying: "I do not accept the moral teachings of the Bible (or whatever other religious book you care to mention) on the subject of homosexuality" and then going on to say: "I do not accept any ethical code at all". If your resistance to "traditional morality" has led you to the rejection of all morality, then you are not likely to find happiness. If your philosophy has become 'I do what I want when I want to whom I want' then disillusion and feelings of emptiness will inevitably follow. Simon Callow, the gay actor, correctly labels such a lifestyle "vacuous hedonism."

The gay scene has a terrible reputation for viciousness, callousness and cynicism. Often in the personal ads you will see people plaintively crying that they are "fed up with the scene" or "need something more than bars and clubs". These people have become sick of the bitchiness and shallowness of their "friends" on the gay scene. They have grown weary of the competition and the emptiness of the constant search for new thrills. While the prime motivation in life is the pursuit of sex, sex and more sex, or the ever more euphoric drug high, then this constant feeling of emptiness will persist.

So many gay men claim that they want to get off the cruising roundabout, the pick-them-up-and-cast-them-off routine that seems so exciting on the surface but which is so harmful in the long term. How many of us have secretly gone into gay bars and hoped that maybe tonight the love of our life will be waiting for us? We find someone who seems to be what we want: genuine, thoughtful and kind (as well as reasonable looking). We go home with him and have a night of wild passion, and in the morning there is an embarrassed moment where he has to tell you that he wants you to leave because he has to go to work or that his cleaning lady is about to arrive. Promises of further contact don't materialise. An embarrassed leave-taking signals another disappointment, and more points on your score card of disillusion.

It works both ways. Many of us have taken home trade that we hoped would amount to more than just an orgasm or two. Or maybe that's all we wanted, and hoped the feeling was mutual. We realise that we don't want to take this any further and want to terminate the arrangement at the first opportunity. It's a difficult situation, and calls for diplomacy and thought for the other person's feelings. But often the only consideration is getting them out of your house and out of your life, as soon as possible.

If you read the quotation from Robert G. Ingersoll which opened this chapter, you will see that in his opinion the way to be happy is to make other people so. This is not a prime consideration on the gay scene. However pleasant and considerate we may be in the rest of our life, once we get on to the club circuit, we rapidly find that the motivating force is sheer sexual gratification, and that alone. People's finer feelings come a poor second. The picture painted by our critics of unsmiling men, hanging around the bar, eyeing each other up, sometimes with an air of desperation to score is not universally true, of course. But then again, it is not entirely unknown, either. We have all been in the kind of dimly lit gay bar whose clients are cruising like mad, unable to smile because the concentration on scoring is so intense. These places used to be known as "meat racks", and not without some justification. Leave your humanity at the door, the penis reigns supreme in such establishments. And as we soon come to realise, the penis does not have a conscience.

Jamie's Story

Jamie has been going to his local gay pub for almost a year now, since he came out. From being thrilled at the prospect that this establishment seemed to offer, he has gradually come to hate it. Yet he still goes there each weekend in the hope that something different will happen.

> I used to go to the bar every Saturday night, dressed up to the nines and thinking I was the best thing since sliced bread. There were lots of great-looking guys there, and I had this fantasy that one of them would see me and think 'This is the boy for me' and we'd settle down and have a happy life together. I don't consider myself to be fabulous looking, but I'm young and I work out and look after my body, and that seemed to appeal to a lot of them. I never had any problems picking up men who I liked the look of. Sometimes we'd have a really wild time and I'd go on a couple of dates with them, and begin to think it was getting somewhere, and then all of a sudden they'd lose interest. They just wanted to be friends, no strings attached. While I was thinking romance, he was already back in the bar looking for the next prospect. This happened over and over again, and although I've met some decent people, there seems to be this feeling that you need to have sex with someone new every week. I see so many men in there now who I've slept with, and we're on nodding terms, or even on speaking terms, but that's all.

Money, money, money

The commercialisation of our community in recent years has had mixed consequences. It has brought many new meeting places and safe, high-quality venues for our entertainment. But the result of that has been a severe reduction in non-commercial community facilities. The annual Pride celebration changed from being a voluntary, community celebration of our diversity into a commercialised event of gargantuan proportions. It went bankrupt a couple of times and one year it didn't happen at all. There is now no community centre in London, as there is in Edinburgh, Manchester and a few other regional towns.

Those who wanted a gay community that is welcoming and inclusive have lost the battle. We've voted with our feet and created 'gay villages' in London and Manchester which seem to revolve mostly around hedonistic indulgence.

As Chris Woods said in his pamphlet *State of the Queer Nation* (Cassell, 1995): "Not everyone is buying into this new commercialism. Once described as 'the longest catwalk in the world', Soho's Old Compton Street is not the heart of the gay ghetto, but an extension on to the pavement of the least pleasant values of the clubs and bars. To walk down this street is not to be part of a nascent community, but to be judged against the markers of the new commercialism. Is he or she dressed right? Do they look and act the part? Are they an 'acceptable' homosexual? Can they afford to play? It is not surprising that some gay and lesbian Londoners will go out of their way to avoid taking this vacuous passage. Many are alienated from the current scene, whether for aesthetic, political or financial reasons."

Sex in Public

Then comes the tricky topic of public sex. Sex in cottages, on heaths and beaches and in alleyways. It seems as popular as ever, despite the fact that we have hundreds of legitimate meeting places now. The allure of cruising may be that it lacks the competitiveness of the gay bar—you don't necessarily have to be young or good looking to get sex in a lavatory. You don't even have to define yourself as gay. Those who would be laughed out of a trendy gay bar because of their age, their thick glasses or their club foot may still be able to score in the local cottage. So long as they don't want romance or conversation, they should manage an orgasm.

But the appeal seems to be more than that. Some men who are successful on the commercial gay scene still find time to search for sex in public cruising spots, too. Mostly cottagers are discreet, but occasionally an unsuspecting heterosexual will happen upon a couple—or more—men engaged in gay sex in a public toilet or in some bushes, and they will complain. At that point the police become involved and the whole thing becomes very nasty. And sometimes the police themselves act as agents provocateurs, even though they've promised not to do so.

Then the justifications begin to pour out of the fans of public sex. Straights are hung-up about it, they say, they have no right to try to stop us doing whatever we want, wherever we want. They should stay away from toilets if they aren't interested, it's a part of traditional gay culture etc. etc.

There is outrage from some elements of the gay community that anyone should even dare to object to the sleazy goings-on in public. If they don't want their children to see men fucking or fellating each other, they cry, they should keep them out of the park. Let them play on the road! These same men object to the police trying to move such activities out of the parks and into more appropriate places, such as gay saunas.

I am not saying that cruising does not have a place in some people's lives, desperate as they are and rejected as they are by the commercial milieu, but some cruising grounds have taken on almost institutional proportions and have become veritable no-go areas for straight people. This is not acceptable. It does our dignity no good and it does our cause no good. But then, when people live totally for their own gratification, the needs of others always take second place.

But let's be realistic. Gay men are men, and men have pressing sexual needs which are more easily aroused and swiftly gratified than those of women. They have less need for an emotional element in their pursuit of pure sexual gratification.

The journalist Carol Sarler put it this way, when commenting (for a straight audience) in *The Sunday People* about an MP who had been caught cruising for sex on some heathland: "What is it about gay men and casual sex with strangers? I suggest it's nothing to do with gay and everything to do with men. And that the only reason heterosexual men don't rampage in the bushes is that there would be no point: THEIR chosen sexual partners—women—have far too much innate taste and integrity to join in. Don't believe me? Ask yourself this: if your chap knew he could head for the hills, and there find 100 girlies offering free sex with no commitment (not even dinner to buy!), wouldn't you have to nail his feet to the floor?"

Without the constraining influence of women, gay men have found that sex is available more or less whenever they want it. They just have to ask. Both participants in gay sex are likely to be equally quick to arousal, and similarly rapidly satisfied from an orgasmic viewpoint. That's fair enough when both participants are consenting adults. But if the pursuit of the orgasm is the be-all and end-all of people's love lives, it will rapidly become unfulfilling. It is at this point that the new thrill has to be sought. New excitements and novelties have to be tried. Drugs make their entrance, and wilder sexual practices such as bondage, sado-masochism, fist-fucking and water sports. Jaded men need to ratchet the whole experience higher and higher, and eventually it becomes a self-destructive pursuit that brings misery and decay.

In the gay community S&M and other way-out practices are not only approved of, they are positively encouraged. All around us in our media and in our places of recreation we see images of men in chains and leather and rubber, having sex that is full of violence and hatred (albeit simulated). We are encouraged to believe that this is normal, natural and just another way of expressing our sexuality. We are not encouraged to think about what it represents.

Those who dare object to this degrading parade of water sports and coprophilia, whipping and torture, are called small-minded and uptight. But if we ask our lovers to shit on us, or to tie us up and torture us, what can it signify about our relationships? And where does it go from there? And yet we are pushed into imagining that such activities are the everyday stuff of gay life. When a group of gay men were brought to court for practising sado-masochism on each other (an operation the police code-named Spanner), the gay community rallied to their defence. Everyone was agreed that state interference in the private, consenting lives of adults was wrong, and what these consenting adults did to each other in private should not have been a matter for the law. But that was not the same as approving those activities. As Chris Woods wrote: "Support does not extend to wholesale endorsement of either S&M or everything it might entail. When we discuss S&M, the predominant image presented by the gay media is one of highly stylised and ritualised sex acts performed by mature men and women, fully conversant with the consequences of their actions. For many S&Mers, this is less than true. The Spanner defendants did not, on the whole, represent the sophisticated urban coterie. Instead it was made up of middle-aged, pre-liberation males, some of whom despised themselves so much that their pursuit of S&M was an attempt at self-obliteration. ... In endorsing without question the Spanner campaign, we risk losing touch with the reasons why many are drawn into S&M, and the damage it might do."

There has to be more to life...

If we want to be happy, we have to look honestly at the way we are living. Peggy Lee once sang a song entitled "Is that all there is?" It might well qualify as the anthem of many gay men who have become addicted to thoughtless self-gratification.

Well, there *can* be more. Much more. But if we are to find happiness as gay men we are going to have to start thinking about some kind of ethical code. It doesn't have to be the 'traditional' version based on religion that brings so much misery and disapproval, but it does have to involve some kind of awareness of the needs of other people.

Situational ethics is a philosophy the basis of which is that moral decisions have to be made in the light of the circumstances in which we find ourselves. Naturally, this has been blamed for the state we find ourselves in now. The decisions so many gay men make are based on their personal circumstances, but are geared towards their own pleasure without thought for the consequences. Ted, for instance, might have the hots for Alan, who just happens to be his best-friend Doug's long-term lover. One day Ted finds himself alone with Alan, and decides to make a move. His motivation is pure lust. He has no desire to take Alan away from Doug, just to have sex with him. He knows that it will cause trouble between all three of them—Doug has told him proudly that his and Alan's relationship is monogamous, something which is important to him. But Ted goes ahead anyway because— well, he wants to. He gives no thought to the way Doug might react when he finds out—will he be hurt, will he feel betrayed, jealous, angry? What does Ted care? He just wants to see what Alan has in his pants!

Every man for himself, you might say. If Ted and Alan want to do it, why not?

Well, because of Doug, that's why not.

In Robert G. Ingersoll's philosophy "The place to be happy is here, the time to be happy is now" and that seems to say it's OK to do whatever comes into your head, so long as there's the possibility of getting away with it. But Ingersoll's qualification is "the way to be happy is to make others so", and in this little scenario someone is going to be very unhappy. In the long term maybe all of them are going to be unhappy—Doug because he was betrayed, Alan because he betrayed the person he cares for and Ted because he loses the friendship of them both. Happiness cannot necessarily be equated with instant gratification of every whim. Happiness can sometimes come from restraint and self-discipline.

But, you might say, it's the same for straight people. The incidence of adultery isn't exactly insignificant. They're always doing the dirty on each other! It's true that straight people betray each other's trust, too, but generally the idea of adultery is disapproved of in straight society, and generally affairs are conducted secretively and with lots of attendant guilt. In gay society such betrayal is considered the norm, and guilt is frequently nowhere to be seen.

Making an ethical code for ourselves

In their book *After the Ball* (Plume (USA), 1990) Marshall Kirk and Hunter Madsen give a devastating critique of what is wrong with gay life, and why so many gay men are unhappy. They say that the community that we have created for ourselves is rather similar to what the world would be like if it were run by six year old boys. It is chaotic and selfish. They cite gay men who continue to have unsafe sex, even though they know they are HIV positive, and the irresponsible behaviour of other men on the bar and club scene. They conclude that we must embrace some kind of moral code. If we don't, we will deny ourselves—and each other—happiness, and we will continue to incite the disapproval of the straight community.

The first rule of situational ethics—the so-called Golden Rule—is very simple:

Treat other people the way you want them to treat you.

It is an insight that has occurred independently to moralists and thinkers throughout the ages, from Confucius in ancient China to present-day Europe, from every major religion to humanists. The reason it has figured so frequently throughout the history of thought and philosophy is because it makes such good sense. If we apply this one simple injunction to all our decisions, we will find that the world will become a better place.

Naturally, not everyone is going to treat you in the way you'd like them to. There will still be those who will reject you if you aren't gorgeous, who will try to belittle you because it makes them feel better, who will be cynical and exploitative in their dealings with their fellow gays. But the circle of nastiness has to be broken somewhere, and it has to start with individuals. We all have to make the decision to treat each other with more respect. Even if we aren't attracted physically to someone, it doesn't mean that we are entitled to be hard and cruel to them. We are not entitled to put other people or ourselves at risk of HIV by ignoring safer sex. Drugs and drink may provide temporary props—momentary feelings of euphoria and well-being—but they are not happiness.

Be your own master in this respect as in all others. Make your own decisions about how to behave, and don't take other people's behaviour as your yardstick. Make for yourself the decision to be respectful and accepting of people in all their variety. This is going to be difficult to put into practice, but it's worth a try. Perhaps, when we're out and about on the scene, we can make the decision to stop treating each other totally as disposable sex toys. It doesn't mean that we have to restrict our sex lives, we can still be raunchy and uninhibited, and, if both parties are consenting, we can have sex for its own sake. But if we don't want to pursue that person, then we can end the association with a little more gentleness. We can bring real loyalty to our friendships instead of convenience loyalty, the kind that can be disposed of when it doesn't suit us.

Pollyana-ish idealism? Maybe. But if we all made the decision to behave a little more thoughtfully and a little less selfishly, we might find the quality of our gay lives improved no end.

There are plenty of good, honest, considerate and kind people in gay life. But when we get involved in the ruthlessly competitive world of the gay sexual market place, it can be a depressing and destructive experience. As we've already said, our penises do not have consciences, and therefore we can't let them dictate the direction of our lives. We have to constrain our sexual impulses to a degree, with simple concerns for our own safety and the safety of others. If we decide to live by some ethical code which demands that we take responsibility for our actions, then the search for happiness as a homosexual will be a little easier.

9: Some other issues

Older gay men

There are now nearly 9 million people over the age of 65 in Britain, and if we assume an incidence of around 2.5%, something like 200,000 of them must be lesbian or gay. Despite the rising numbers, there are still almost as many misunderstandings about the lives of older gay men inside the gay community as there are outside it. We all know the caricature of the lonely old queen—embittered, isolated and pitied, crying out for sex but excluded from the sexual market place by dint of advancing years. And yet almost all the research carried out into the lives of older gay men paints a very different picture—many of the more mature among us have a much more interesting life than is generally realised. As the researchers Bell and Weinberg found in their book *Male Homosexuals: their problems and adaptations*: "Our data suggest that in some respects our older homosexuals have a greater well-being than our younger homosexuals." Another American survey of gay men over fifty showed that the majority of them were satisfied with their life, felt that they were not deprived of sexual opportunity and considered that there were some distinct advantages to being mature.

You shouldn't become too discouraged if you are an older gay man who is fresh to the gay world and imagine that everything revolves around young people. It doesn't. Many older people have acquired for themselves a small, but beloved, circle of friends who satisfy all their needs. However if you are new to gay life and have not already established a network, it may take some time and a little effort to get things started. It takes persistence, courage and a bit of luck, too. You can help yourself along by severely restricting the use of such phrases as "I'm too old for that" or "That's only for younger people". While it is probably a waste of time trying to compete against the young dudes in the sexual market place, age should not be used as an excuse not to try new things. If you want to be a happy *older* homosexual, you'll have to be prepared to make as many adjustments as the younger people, maybe even more. Just bear in mind that you have in your favour the head start of experience, contacts and confidence.

If you want to meet other gay people of your own age, you could think about going along to one of the gay groups specifically set up for the more mature among us. See the listings in the gay press for latest information. You'll find these groups welcoming and warm.

Older men's sexual urges don't disappear, but problems for some include a lessening of potency and difficulties with sexual performance because of weakening physical health. As we become older, some of the nerve pathways become a little sluggish and responses might not be as quick and ready as they once were. There may be other explanations for these problems: some of the drugs that are used to treat the diseases of older people can interfere with the ability to get an erection, as can tranquillisers and anti-depressants. Both diabetes and anaemia can also cause impotence, and arthritis and rheumatism can make sexual activity difficult. But with a little imagination, limited physical capabilities can be compensated for by a less physically demanding, but still emotionally satisfying, sex life. Don't underestimate the joy of cuddling.

Aids, too, can still be a problem for older gay men. All the safer sex advice which has gone before is applicable to anyone who is still sexually active. The medical establishment has failed to take into account the sexual activities of older gay men and many education campaigns completely ignore them. The number of those over 50 who are becoming HIV positive is increasing at an alarming rate. There can be no slackening of vigilance.

For many, the mature years have brought with them a more relaxed and less stressful attitude to their sexuality. Others, though, have never really managed to prise the closet door open and remain "discreet" until the day they die. It can be difficult, as they come to depend more and more on other people, to have the courage to come out to them if they are likely to react unsympathetically. A long lifetime of denial can be difficult to shake off.

Other men have found that their later years have been the most satisfying, and that they have felt that after their career was over, there was no good reason to stay in the closet. Much of what has been said in the earlier chapters will apply to this group. There is no need to be lonely and isolated. There are plenty of groups and organisations which will welcome the input of those with experience and enthusiasm, and who have time on their hands.

For those very old gay men who may need to live in a nursing or retirement home or sheltered housing, there may be problems of acceptance by the staff or other residents or neighbours. At present there is little support in this area, but the problem is being addressed by various groups who hope to raise consciousness of the needs of older gay people in community care.

Alcoholism and drugs

Because so much of gay life revolves around pubs and clubs, there is the ever-present danger that alcohol will become more than just a pleasant relaxant. Addiction can creep up on people with surprising stealth. For gay people having trouble and conflict in their life, drink might appear to provide an easy escape from the pain. Indeed, there is some research to indicate that some gay men can't even think about having sex unless they are under the influence of drink or drugs.

Naturally, tackling the underlying problems is the best way to get drink under control, but in the meantime watch out for these tell-tale signs:

- The need to drink every day, whatever the circumstances
- Drinking on your own, on a regular basis
- Drinking in the morning in order to steady yourself
- Finding you can't remember the events of a previous night's drinking session
- Becoming annoyed when people criticise your drinking.
- Feeling guilty or bad about your drinking

Given that alcohol plays such a large part in gay life, what is a reasonable amount to drink? The amounts recommended as "safe" by the medical royal colleges are twenty-one units per week for men and fourteen units for women (a unit is half a pint of normal strength beer, a small glass of wine or a single pub-size tot of spirits—whisky, gin, vodka etc.) It is important to have days off from drinking in order to give the body a chance to recover from the poisoning which alcohol induces. This does not mean that it is OK to drink the whole of your allowance on a Saturday night and then abstain for the rest of the week. Large intakes of alcohol at one go can increase the damage to the stomach; you are also more likely to have accidents when you're stoned out of your head. The liver requires on average seventy-two hours to recover from a dose of alcohol, so the answer must be that it is better to drink a little from time to time than it is to go on occasional benders.

Research has shown that some people's health—mainly middle-aged men and elderly women—can benefit from a couple of drinks a day. Red wine in particular, it is thought, may give some protection from heart disease. However, this does not mean that drinking to excess is good for you—more than a couple of drinks a day and you might find yourself suffering the consequences of other drink-related problems.

And before you shrug this off as being inapplicable to you, bear in mind that 40% of hospital beds in Britain are taken up by alcohol-related conditions.

Before you can help yourself with a drink problem you have to admit you've got it. Be realistic in your assessment and listen carefully if someone close to you is sending out warning signals—they can often see clearly what is not obvious to you.

Here are ten suggestions for taking control of your drinking:

1. *Keep a drink diary*
    Write down when and how much you drink and how any resolve to "cut down" is progressing.
2. *Stick to the limit you have set*
    Work out a reasonable limit, both for day-to-day life and special occasions.
3. *Be careful at home*
    Most people pour larger drinks at home than they are given in a pub.
4. *Don't be afraid to say no*
    Don't let anyone pressure you into drinking. Plan your excuses in advance.
5. *Avoid rounds*
    Round buying often means you drink more than you want. Skip some rounds. Buy your own drinks or choose an alcohol-free drink.
6. *Pace your drinks*
    Choose smaller drinks and drink them slowly. Intersperse them with soft drinks.
7. *Occupy yourself*
    Find something else to do while you drink to distract you—eat, chat, play darts or pool.
8. *Find alternatives*
    Don't drink because you're bored, stressed or upset. Look for other ways to relax.
9. *Have a day off*
    After drinking heavily, avoid alcohol for a day or two to give your body time to recover. Having days off proves you are in control.
10. *Reward yourself*
    Be pleased with your will-power and self-control, but also be honest with yourself.

If you've reached the stage where you know you aren't in control of your intake of alcohol and have accepted that you need help, contact Alcoholics Anonymous or Accept. They often run groups especially for gay people, and their local branch will let you know if there is one operating in your area. Alternatively, ring a gay help line. It is an unfortunate fact that alcoholism is becoming a problem for an increasing number of gay people, and the tragedy is that they are often unaware it is happening to them. There are support groups for those who live with alcoholics, too. Al-anon is one of these.

Drugs

Illegal drug-taking is now very much a part of the commercial gay scene. Ecstasy, cannabis, amphetamines, cocaine, LSD, heroin, barbiturates and other substances are available in many night clubs and pubs and a significant sub-culture has grown up around them. Research shows that gay people take far more drugs than their straight equivalents—often several varieties at the same time and over longer periods. Straight drug-users tend to do most of their experimenting in their twenties and then give up in order to take care of families and other responsibilities. With fewer such constraints, gay drug-users tend to continue taking drugs well into middle age.

If you socialise on the gay scene for a while you'll probably hear people boasting about the great highs they've had, and the way they use drugs as a sort of prop which helps them do things they wouldn't otherwise be able to do. What regular users don't tell you about are the dreadful downers they've had, the unhappiness they're trying to escape through drug use or the horrendous cost of supporting their habit.

Most drugs have side-effects, some of them dangerous or even fatal when taken in excess. Most of these drugs will interfere with the speed of your reactions and can make it difficult or dangerous for you to drive or use other machinery. Some substances make you anxious, depressed or aggressive. There is no guarantee, either, that you are getting what you pay for. Sometimes the drugs bought illicitly are adulterated with sugar, laxatives or cheaper, more dangerous, drugs. You can never be sure how strong the pill is you're taking or what exactly it is you are injecting into your arm. Mixing drugs can produce a lethal cocktail.

These are some of the substances you might come across if you frequent the gay scene.

Ecstasy or "E"

This comes in tablet form or different coloured capsules or powder. It also goes under other names such as 'dennis the menace', 'rhubarb and custard', 'new yorkers', 'love doves', 'disco burgers' or 'phase 4'. Ecstasy can induce a feeling of friendliness and extra energy for a while, but as it wears off you are likely to feel pretty rotten. Taken in larger amounts, it can produce feelings of anxiety, confusion or paranoia. If used regularly it can interfere with sleep. It should certainly be avoided by anyone who suffers from epilepsy or who has a heart condition.

If it is taken in a hot atmosphere, such as a disco, it can cause heat-stroke. It will destroy brain cells and, with prolonged use, can damage the liver. Several deaths have already been associated with its use. Although it is not addictive, it *is* illegal, and can be dangerous. Don't ever take more than one E at a time (after a while the body builds up a tolerance which might tempt you to increase the dose—don't do it), and don't take it in conjunction with alcohol. If you're taking E, make sure that you take plenty of non-alcoholic drinks to prevent dehydration. It is almost inevitable that you will have a hangover the following day, sometimes this can be quite severe and you may find that you are losing days from work or studies as a result. Being caught in possession of E can lead to a large fine and a criminal record.

Cocaine or coke (also known as 'snow', 'rock' and 'base')

This is a powerful stimulant which is sometimes injected but more often sniffed through a tube into the nose and absorbed into the blood supply. Cocaine produces feelings of exhilaration and euphoria and an indifference to pain. You may feel strong and invulnerable. These feelings can rapidly turn into panic and anxiety.

The effects soon peak and then lessen rapidly. You will need to take more and more in order to achieve the same effect and this can lead to dependence. Then comes sickness, sleeplessness and weight loss. "Crack" is a cheaper version of cocaine, treated with chemicals so it can be smoked. The initial high is followed by unpleasant after-effects, but users can rapidly become dependent.

LSD (also known as 'acid')

LSD is a man-made substance, minute quantities of which are impregnated on to blotting paper and then dissolved on the tongue. Quite often substances sold as LSD contain none of the drug at all. The "trip" begins after about half an hour, and fades after about twelve hours, depending on how much you've taken. The effects depend very much on the mood you are in, as well as the dose. Your vision and hearing may become distorted and there may be a feeling of being outside your body. Bad trips can be particularly unpleasant with depression, dizziness, hallucinations and extreme anxiety. These are more likely if the user is already feeling anxious or is in unfamiliar surroundings.

Heroin (also known as 'smack', 'junk', 'H' and 'skag')

Heroin is made from the opium poppy. In its purest form it is a white powder which can be sniffed, smoked or injected. Heroin depresses brain activity, widens blood vessels (giving a feeling of warmth) and causes constipation. It can create feelings of total relaxation and pleasure. It makes people drowsy, with feelings of warmth and contentment. This all sounds fine, but unfortunately that is only the start of the problem. Once physical dependence has been established, the desire to get hold of the drug can be desperate. There are enough Hollywood films about the consequences of drug-taking for us to know what lengths addicts will go to for their next fix. Unless they have large amounts of money, users will eventually have to resort to lying, deceit, betrayal and crime in order to get the next fix. And each fix will need to be bigger than the last.

Overdosing results in unconsciousness, coma and sometimes death from breathing failure. If you take other drugs, such as alcohol, at the same time as cocaine, the chances of your dying are increased. Repeated injection by users causes damage to the body. Often it is injected with dirty needles, increasing the chance of acquiring HIV. After a while, apathy overwhelms the victim and self-neglect, poor diet and indifference ensure a miserable existence.

Cannabis (also called 'dope', 'blow', 'wacky backy', 'grass', 'shit' and 'hash')

Cannabis comes from the plant *cannabis sativa*. It is generally rolled with tobacco and smoked as a cigarette. It takes effect very quickly after being inhaled, causing users to feel more relaxed and talkative. Cannabis is not addictive, but, as with tobacco, it can damage the lungs if smoked frequently. It is not a good idea to drive after using cannabis. A case has been made for the legalisation of cannabis, its proponents arguing that it is far less damaging than some legal substances such as tobacco and alcohol. It is probably the most widely-used of the proscribed drugs.

Poppers

Other substances which you'll come across in the gay world—and which aren't illegal—are amyl nitrate and butyl nitrate, commonly called "poppers". These are popular with gay men because of their supposed aphrodisiac properties. Amyl was developed to help people with angina. When an attack came on, the sufferer would snap one of the small glass capsules and sniff the contents—thus "poppers". Amyl nitrate dilates the veins and causes a rush of blood to the head resulting in a kind of euphoria. The effects last only a few seconds and it is usually sniffed at the moment of orgasm.

Some research shows that poppers might be dangerous, and they should certainly be avoided by stroke victims or anyone with weak kidneys, heart disease, liver trouble, circulatory problems, asthma or emphysema. A number of doctors are convinced that poppers play an important part in the development of Aids, and they should certainly be strictly avoided by those who are HIV positive. Amyl is not addictive, but the effects of long-term use are unknown.

These are the facts about drugs, and you should think about them carefully before getting involved in the drug scene—even on a casual, occasional basis. At base it is a sordid, exploitative, crime-ridden world and contact with it will impede, if not completely stall, your push to be a happy homosexual.

The dance culture—which is one of the great pleasures of gay life for many young people—has as its constant companion the drug culture. But you can choose to separate them—or at least live by the old maxim "Moderation in all things". Never forget that, as in all areas of your personal life, you always have a choice.

Bereavement

Bereavement has become a depressingly familiar experience for many gay people. Aids has robbed us of friends long before their time, and it is particularly hard to accept the death of young people. This ghastly problem is being addressed by the proliferating specialist gay bereavement groups. The counsellors in these groups are familiar with the special circumstances surrounding the death of someone from Aids and of the particular needs of gay people who are trying to cope with their loss.

The effects can be particularly harsh on a surviving partner, particularly if he (even subconsciously) blames his partner—or himself—for the premature death. Almost inevitably, some of his friends and relatives will not have been aware of the relationship and the bereaved person might have difficulty finding the support he needs at such a time.

Families who did not approve of the relationship have been known to exclude gay partners from the funeral, and bereaved partners have often experienced difficulty in getting time off work: compassionate leave does not seem to extend to "just friends". If there is no will, families can step in to claim the property of the dead person and generally pile agony on top of the tragedy.

To help protect themselves against the possibility of these events happening, gay partners should:

* Make wills. The importance of this cannot be overstated. A lawyer will do it relatively cheaply. A gay help line will be able to refer you to a sympathetic legal adviser, or see advertisements in the gay press. Name your partner as 'executor' of your will—this means that legally your partner has final say about the funeral arrangements and gives him some control over the administration of the estate (subject to the provisions of the will).
* Name your partner as next of kin if one of you goes into hospital. This will overcome the problem of restricted visiting should anything go wrong. If you fear an adverse reaction from hospital staff, describe him as "a friend".
* Seek counselling from a gay help line as soon after bereavement as possible. They can help you in practical as well as emotional ways. The Lesbian and Gay Bereavement Project runs a telephone help line offering advice and support to people bereaved by the death of a same-sex partner, or otherwise affected by bereavement. All their volunteers are well-trained and skilled at helping you come to terms with your feelings.

Mourning and grief are very important elements of recovery from the pain of bereavement. It is often difficult for those who are not gay themselves to accept the depth of feeling which can be present in gay love, and so it might be wise to seek solace among other gay people.

Young gays

Generally the age of consent law is not a great consideration in the lives of young gay people, even though it does discriminate against them. However, the threat of prosecution by parents unhappy with relationships that are technically illegal has been used to frighten some sons into returning home. The law is based on the assumption that young people need to be protected from what are seen as predatory adult homosexuals. Is this true or fair?

In Germany, a large-scale study of nearly 800 homosexual men was conducted by researchers Reiche and Dannecker of Frankfurt University. They said:

> In our empirical study...we could show that about 30% of subjects had their first homosexual experience before the age of eighteen, and that they involved a partner who himself was not older than eighteen. Only 34% of our subjects had their first homosexual experience before the age of eighteen with a partner who was eighteen or over. Apart from the fact that there is no such thing as seduction into homosexuality, it is also clear that another common supposition is wrong; the supposition that normally the first homosexual experience would take place between an older man, supposed to be a homosexual, and a juvenile...The initial thesis that the genesis of homosexuality can be attributed to seduction by adults is, therefore, empirically wrong.

Young gay people living at their parents' home might be financially dependent on them, and the effects of this dependence can be very oppressive. Some young gay people who have left home and become involved in a homosexual affair have actually been taken into care by local authorities following complaints by parents.

Only by a process of education and positive example will young gay people find the confidence to assert their rights. Teachers who might provide a positive role model for gay pupils are obliged to stay in the closet in order to protect their jobs. Educational materials on homosexuality aimed at young people are very hard to find in schools. A young gay Londoner is quoted in one report as saying the only book he could find in the school library that mentioned homosexuality was the Bible.

There are gay youth groups springing up, but they are few and far between. Most universities and colleges now have a gay society, and it's worth checking if there is one in your area. They nearly always welcome non-students to their events. See the gay press for full details.

Some young people live in abusive homes and, in an attempt to escape, find themselves living on the streets, which provides yet another soul-destroying environment for them to live in. There is some help at hand in the shape of the Albert Kennedy Trust, a Manchester based charity which aims to help homeless gay teenagers find accommodation. Despite limited funding, it tries to provide a nation-wide service, placing teenagers made homeless as a result of their sexuality with carefully vetted lesbian and gay carers. The young people can then begin to rebuild their lives with the help of positive role models. The Albert Kennedy Trust gets referrals not only from Social Services departments, but from children's homes. Their address and contact number and those of some youth groups are in the back of this book.

Married gay men

It has been said that the majority of gay men are invisible because they are married. There is little doubt that many hundreds of thousands of our number do opt for the heterosexual institution, and they do so for many reasons: sometimes it's an attempt to escape the truth of their own sexuality, some of them are truly bisexual and can make relationships with either men or women; some of these will use marriage as a "front", a parody of respectability which acts as a cover for their real activities. Sometimes it is a considered decision because they don't want to define themselves as gay and accept the marginalisation which this will bring. Some of the time it is simply to fulfil the expectations of other people. Pressure from family, peers—and religion—can be extremely strong. Recent research in America in relation to Aids indicates that the majority of men who engage in homosexual sex "very often" or "occasionally" still marry at least once. The researchers go so far as to say that there is no such thing as an "exclusive homosexual".

There are nearly always tensions in a marriage involving a gay partner. It often happens that when marriages are entered into, gay feelings are vague and, it is hoped, can be ignored. Later they may become more insistent and demand expression. Then, when the homosexuality of one of the marriage partners is revealed, it can result in the marriage ending. But more often than is realised, the straight partner is prepared to compromise and accept new terms for the relationship.

A leaflet, prepared by a group which specialises in helping the straight partners of gay men, said: "Many of us have been able to re-negotiate our marriage contracts so that both ourselves and our husbands can lead a fuller and happier life in which we can share our concern for each other."

So, although marriage can be a disaster, it doesn't have to be. There are alternatives, as many people have discovered.

And just because a person has homosexual sex, it doesn't necessarily mean that he will define himself as homosexual. There are endless possibilities along the sexual spectrum, and we are all capable of change throughout our lives. Perhaps, as some people would like, we should stop defining ourselves as homosexual or heterosexual and simply say we are people, and that we will love whoever we choose.

The gay press
The gay community has managed to build an effective communications system for itself, despite much opposition.

In Britain there are several news magazines and free newspapers which report developments relevant to gay people, from a gay point of view. It was a long time before the major newsagents would distribute *Gay Times*, but now it is available throughout the country. You can subscribe, of course, if you find it difficult to pay for your favourite gay magazine at the counter. *Gay Times* is a serious long-standing magazine which examines aspects of gay life and culture, as well as bringing news and comment about what is happening in relation to homosexuals. It also contains a great deal of essential information for those looking for an entry on to either the voluntary or the commercial gay scene.

The freesheets such as *The Pink Paper* and *Boyz* are available from gay outlets such as bars, clubs and bookshops. They can also be obtained on subscription. *The Pink Paper* is a source of news and information, while *Boyz* concerns itself with the sex, club, bar and entertainment scene. A "lifestyle" magazine with a gay slant is *Attitude*, also available from newsagents.

As well as news coverage, gay papers can educate and encourage thought about the many implications of being gay. The feature pages explore gay life from many angles and frequently offer writing of high standard. There is also entertainment, and listings of events and meeting places that are essential for those starting out on acquiring a social life. You'll find everything from contacts for gay groups, holiday firms, book shops, mortgage brokers, to special interest groups, pubs and clubs. There are also hundreds of personal ads.

Many countries in the Western world now have a well-established gay press, and it is invaluable in ensuring that our sense of solidarity, community and concern for each other is consolidated.

Gay people with disabilities

The problems of people with disabilities can be doubly hard. The isolation and loneliness can be especially severe if mobility is restricted. Like the rest of society, able-bodied gays have a long way to go in acknowledging the special and pressing needs of those with disabilities. Work has started, though, to raise people's awareness of the importance of making special facilities available to all gay people.

Unfortunately, many groups have to meet in the upstairs rooms of pubs or places that those with restricted mobility might find difficulty in reaching. This shouldn't be an absolute bar to less able members taking an active part in other events. With a little planning and forethought, some kind of arrangement can often be made—perhaps it is simply a matter of making group members aware of any special needs. Those of us who don't have difficulties should guard against complacency and thoughtlessness about others who might need assistance.

There are groups that have been set up to look into these problems, and to campaign for better facilities. They also support gay people who are experiencing difficulties because of their disability. So, if you think such a group would be appropriate to you, please get in touch with them. They often have pen friend lists and counselling facilities as well as practical ways of helping. You'll find some of them listed at the back of this book.

Having a disability is difficult enough for anyone, but being gay and perhaps dependent on the help of others is a significant extra problem. Sometimes carers and helpers prefer not to face up to the sexual needs of those they are helping, which can make coming out even more difficult. But new technology is being applied to help liberate many from complete isolation and dependence. Computers can bring contact with a wide number of others through various networks and e-mail systems. All these avenues are worth investigation. Groups catering for the needs of those with disabilities will be able to give more information. Some of them are listed in the back of this book.

Gays from ethnic minorities

Unfortunately, racism is as deeply rooted in the gay community as it is in the rest of society. Black gays and people from other ethnic minorities in Britain have begun to organise themselves to ensure that their interests are properly represented in the community. They rightly point out that they often suffer prejudice and discrimination not only because of their gayness but also because of their colour. They are likely to encounter homophobia in their family and in their ethnic community, and racism and homophobia in the majority culture. Racism is an issue which will need to be raised and discussed for years to come, and many gay people are challenging their thoughts and feelings on the topic.

Much of what has been written in this book applies to people of all races, but it has to be acknowledged that cultural differences can add significant complications. For example, coming out in a household which is motivated by strong, fundamentalist religious convictions can be extremely difficult, and some cultures have much more severe taboos surrounding homosexuality. Any attempt to come out in such a family-dominated society might lead to ostracism which in turn means the loss of important support structures that help people cope with the racism of the dominant community.

Once again, seeking out specialist groups is the answer. However resistant your family or culture might be to your homosexuality, you can be sure that someone else out there has already been through this particular mill and survived. That doesn't necessarily make it easier for you as an individual, but it might give you the inspiration you need to get started.

Parenting

It is often assumed that all gay men are single or are living with a same-sex lover and do not, therefore, produce children. The truth is that many gay men already have children from previous marriages. Some others have decided that although they do not want a heterosexual relationship, they *do* want the experience of parenting. They have achieved this by a number of means. Some get together with sympathetic lesbians and through Artificial Insemination (in which the woman waits until her fertile time of the month and then introduces the sperm through a syringe), they produce children which they then co-parent. AI is a simple procedure and can be achieved without the help of the medical authorities, and there are books explaining the most successful methods.

A 1990 Act of parliament affecting Great Britain—but not Northern Ireland—regulates such procedures carried out through agencies, but does not cover personal arrangements. New rules about naming the donor father mean that he can legally be traced for maintenance purposes.

The aftermath of parenting arrangements can be complicated. You need to think carefully about the issues before you proceed. How confident are all parties involved that they are going to feel the same way about the arrangement in several years time? What would be the consequence of father and mother falling out at some later date? It would probably pay dividends for anyone contemplating co-parenting to talk to one of the specialist agencies which have been set up to help. You'll find some mentioned in the back of the book. They have had experience of the many complications that can ensue from arrangements such as this, and can warn of the pitfalls.

Some other men have found sympathetic local authorities which allow them to foster—and in some rare cases—adopt children. Usually gay couples, or individuals, will be offered disadvantaged children, often with severe handicaps, which heterosexual couples will not generally be prepared to accept. Taking on such a responsibility is an enormous task, but many gay couples have plunged in and succeeded admirably.

There is prejudice against male adopters and fosterers generally, but if they are also openly gay the odds are stacked against successful applications. However, if it is important to you, then go ahead and try. Many have overcome amazing prejudice in order to be given the privilege of raising children.

Gay parenting is probably the one topic which generates most hostility among heterosexuals, many of whom still subscribe to the notion that gay men must be kept away from children at all costs. Any gay person or couple who tries to break through that prejudice is facing an uphill battle. But unless those battles are fought, we will never progress.

The Law

For all our efforts to achieve equality before the law, there is still a long way to go. And so it is important that every gay person be aware of how the law applies to their life. It is beyond the scope of this book to go into every detail of how the law might affect you—whether in your sexual life or your employment rights or your family life—so it is important that you gain up to date information from reliable sources. Read the gay press for news of developments.

At the time of writing, the law is changing rapidly. The Government has promised that it will lower the age of consent from 18 to 16—equal with that of heterosexuals. By the time this book reaches the shops, we hope that such a change will have reached the statute book. There are intimations that there will be other changes, such as lifting the ban on the entry of gay people into the armed forces, but no firm promises.

If you find you need advice—either because you have fallen foul of the law, or are having dealings with the police, then get advice as soon as possible from a sympathetic lawyer. You will find many of them advertising in the gay press. Some specialise in criminal proceedings, others with civil cases, such as unfair dismissal or disputed wills. There are also organisations, such as Gay Legal Advice Group (GLAD), which can point you in the right direction if you are having problems that may need to be resolved in court or with the help of a solicitor (or GALOP if it involves the police). In each case, contact numbers are shown at the end of the book.

Most gay people are no longer prepared to see themselves as victims, and are much more willing to fight back if they feel they have been unjustly treated. Several cases have reached as far as the European Court of Human Rights, although not all of them have gone in our favour. Now the European Convention on Human Rights has been incorporated into our own domestic law, which raises new hopes that gay people will be able to challenge much of the discrimination that still exists in our legal system.

Gay campaigning

As the gay community becomes ever larger and more diverse, its confidence has increased significantly. There are many people working with great dedication to change the law and to increase social acceptance of homosexuals. They do this in many different ways. The Stonewall Group, for instance, takes the traditional lobbying route, trying to persuade MPs and other influential public figures to make parliamentary changes. It is a long, slow process and many younger gay people are impatient for change—they do not see why they should be on the receiving end of unfair discrimination, and they are angry. Consequently other, more confrontational, groups have formed. Perhaps the best-known of these is OutRage! which describes itself as a "direct action" organisation.

OutRage! organises demonstrations, stunts and imaginative confrontations which aim to bring gay rights a higher profile. They have been very successful in manipulating the media, although some gay people (and a lot of straight ones) regard OutRage! as counterproductive, claiming that it creates hostility rather than understanding.

There are literally hundreds of single-issue groups in the gay community, each working away on a specific aspect of homosexual reform. There are gay groups for members of most of the main political parties, support groups for gay policemen, ex-military personnel, prisoners and so on.

Many local groups work on issues specific to their area— trying to influence local MPs and councils to be more supportive of gay rights and challenging instances of homophobia and discrimination which occur locally. They proved particularly effective during the age of consent campaign in 1994, too, in putting pressure on Members of Parliament.

High profile campaigning isn't everyone's cup of tea, but there are other ways that we can all help in the struggle. Writing letters to the local paper, writing to MPs, complaining about homophobic radio and television broadcasts or newspaper items. As we become personally more confident, making a contribution to the struggle will seem less daunting. There is a great sense of achievement when an objective has been met and often you'll meet interesting new friends in the process.

We can contribute money to those organisations which are fighting for our rights, even if we aren't going to become directly involved. If we could harness all that gay energy, talent, money and determination, our community would be an extremely powerful force. Unfortunately, the option to "pass for straight" is still the one that most gay people go for, and so not only do they not contribute anything to the fight to effect change, they actively undermine other people's efforts by failing to support them.

Which brings us full circle—to come out or not to come out. I think by now you will have realised the emotional and spiritual benefits of doing so, but you may still believe that you will lose out financially or in some other way. In the end, the decision has to be yours.

AND FINALLY...

Having read this book you may imagine that achieving a happy life as a homosexual is far from easy. You'd be right. But I repeat—*it is possible*, and every battle you fight, every stand you take, will make you stronger and more determined.

As you grow in confidence, and meet more people who have succeeded, your self-esteem will increase and it will all become much easier.

Whatever route you choose through gay life—whether alone or as part of a couple, whether defining yourself as gay or queer or bisexual or all these things—you can be sure that wherever you go in the world, you'll find others engaged on the same journey. We all have the battle of finding our identity and, once we have found it, exploring it. It can be a journey full of anxiety and apprehension or it can be one of excitement and joy. You can choose the frame of mind with which you approach each decision you have to make.

Those of our number who have become infected with HIV are also finding new ways of looking at their situation. A new, more optimistic philosophy is developing. People with HIV or Aids are choosing to take control of their lives and to make informed decisions about the treatment they agree to and the alternatives they can explore.

Infection with the virus does not necessarily mean that you are dying, it means that you are living with HIV. Many of the people with Aids have testified that the news of their HIV status has given them a fresh outlook, it has sharpened their sense of life and made them rethink their attitudes to so many things. It is now becoming clear that many people who are HIV positive are going to live for a very long time, and they are going to make the absolute most of that time. Research and development is bowling along at an incredible rate, and new generations of drugs are being developed and tested all the time. There is even renewed optimism that at some point in the not too distant future, a vaccine may be developed that will bring this terrible epidemic to an end.

In the meantime, our knowledge of the virus tells us that if we don't have it already, we can protect ourselves against it. Safer sex is the answer to living a full life without taking foolish risks. If you aren't infected, you need never become infected. If you are infected, you need to protect yourself against other diseases which might threaten your health. Condoms are the answer. Familiarise yourself with rubbers, jack off with johnnys, dabble with Durex. Make condoms as familiar as KY and just as indispensable. Carry them with you everywhere, keep supplies wherever they might be needed. Don't place the responsibility on the other person.

Taking control of your life is a wonderful thing, and having gained control you must make sure that you keep tight hold of the reins. By remembering the golden rule of treating others as we would like them to treat us, we can also ensure that we do not perpetuate the unhappiness and disillusion that blights the lives of so many gay people.

If you are lucky enough to find a partner you want to live with, be sure that the relationship is based on equality. You do not want to jump from one prison to another. Learn about assertiveness, find out how to say the things you want to say, and ask for the things you truly desire, while respecting the needs and desires of other people.

Wherever life leads you, and whatever your future, I wish you success and every happiness.

Useful contacts

There are thousands of gay groups, businesses, agencies and bars throughout the world, so this list is far from exhaustive. However, as a useful starting point, it includes places with a central pool of information. It's almost inevitable that this list will be out of date almost as soon as it is published, and it has not been possible to check out all of the contacts. Some of the magazines mentioned - particularly *Gay Times* - include up-to-date addresses and phone numbers for all local and national facilities. Even if a group in which you are interested is not in your area, if you contact them they may be able to put you in touch with one that is. Also, try looking up "lesbian" or "gay" in your local telephone directory.

Asterisked telephone numbers are expected to change from 22 April 2000 to the bracketed numbers as follows: 0171 (0207); 0181 (0208); 01232 (02690); and 01705 (02392).

HEALTH/DISABILITIES/
ALCOHOL

Albany Trust (Relationship &
Psychosexual counselling)
280 Balham High Road
London SW17 7AL
0181-767 1827*

Alcoholics Anonymous
Lesbian and Gay Group
0171-352 3001*

Al-Anon
for partners, family etc. of
problem drinkers,
0171-608 1471*

Blenheim Project
Counselling for drug users
0181-960 5599*
(Mon-Fri 10am-5pm)

Body Positive
(Aids/HIV support and
information)
51b Philbeach Gardens
London SW5 9EB
0171-373 9124*

Deaf Flag
(Federation of Deaf L&G
groups)
7 Victoria Avenue,
South Croydon,
Surrey CR2 0QP

Drinkline
National Alcohol Helpline
0171-332 0202*
(6-11pm)

HEALTH ETC. CONT'D
**Gay & Bisexual Men's Drink
Support Group**
0171-737 3579*

**Gay and Lesbian Mental
Health Service,**
10 Harley Street,
London W1
0171-467 8330*

Group B
for men who have or have had
Hepatitis B
0171-244 6514*

Regard
National lesbian and gay
disabled organisation,
BM Regard, WC1N 3XX
0171-738 8097*

Terrence Higgins Trust
National AIDS organisation
52-54 Grays Inn Rd.
London WC1X 8JU
0171-831 0330*

**UK Coalition for People
Living with HIV & AIDS**
0171-564 2180*

Vigour
Blind & Partially Sighted gays
Keith May 01705-524739*

PARENTS, FAMILIES
**Families and Friends of
Lesbians and Gays (FFLAG),**
0161-628 7621 and
0171-791 2854*

Happy Families
c/o Community House,
7 Nether Hall Road,
Doncaster DN1 2PH
01302-361319

Parents Friend
support for the parents of gay
people c/o V.A. Leeds, Stringer
House, 34 Lupton Street,
Hunslet, Leeds LS10 2QW
Joy/Alan 0113-267 4627
or Val 0113-257 7523

Parents Together
PO Box 464
London SE25 4AT
0181-650 5268*

Positive Parenting
Support for lesbian and gay
foster and adoptive families
Dep. 7, 1 Newton Street,
Manchester M1 1HW

GENERAL HELPLINES,
CENTRES & BOOKSHOPS
At Ease
confidential service for all
armed forces
28 Commercial Street
London E1 6LS
0171-247 5164 (Sun 5-7pm)*

Bisexual Helpline
0181-569 7500*
Tues & Wed 7.0-9.30pm

**Cardiff Lesbian, Gay &
Bisexual Phoneline**
01222-398 903*

GEN. ADVICE CONT.
Cara-Friend (Belfast)
PO Box 44, Belfast BT1 1SH
01232-322 023*

Edinburgh Gay Switchboard
0131-556 4049 (7.30-10pm)

FRIEND
Befriending and counselling
group, 86 Caledonian Road,
London N1 9DN
Helpline (L+G)
0171-837 3337*

Gay Legal Advice (GLAD)
0171-837 5212*
(Mon-Thur 7-9.30 pm)

**Gay London Policing Group
(GALOP)**
Confidential advice and
support in connection with
homophobic violence and the
police.
0171-704 2040*

Gay Outdoor Club
Groups for various outdoor
activities nationwide, also has
women's group. Send A5 s.a.e.
to: GOC, PO Box 16124,
Glasgow G12 9YT
0141-334 0812

Gay Times
Ground Floor,
Worldwide House
116-134 Bayham Street
London NW1 0BA
(see next column)

National monthly news
magazine available from
newsagents or by subscription.

Gay's the Word
Lesbian and Gay Bookshop
66 Marchmont Street
London WC1N 1AB
Mail order service available

Gay Scotland
58a Broughton Street,
Edinburgh EH1 3SA
Monthly magazine covering
the whole of Scotland.

**Lesbian and Gay
Bereavement Project**
0181-455 8894*

**Lesbian and Gay
Employment Rights,
(LAGER)**
Unit 1G, Leroy House,
436 Essex Road
London N1 3QP
0171-704 8066*

**Lesbian and Gay National
Pen Pals**
Free e-mail service
http://www.angelfire.com/in/
horwich/index.html

**London Lesbian and Gay
Switchboard**
Tel: 0171-837 7324*
24-hour information and advice
service. Useful source for all
information, but very busy.

Manchester Lesbian & Gay Centre
49-51 Sidney Street
0161-274 3814

Northern Ireland Gay Rights Association (NIGRA)
PO Box 44,
Belfast BT1 1SH
01232-664111*

Out! Bookshop,
4/7 Dorest Street,
Brighton
01273-623356

Out-Side-In
(Volunteer support for gays in prison)
PO Box 119.
Orpington,
Kent BR6 9ZZ

Pink Paper
Cedar House,
72 Holloway Road,
London N7 8NZ
Weekly freesheet available nationally in pubs and clubs.
Also available on subscription.

Polari (Raising visibility on housing, care etc. for older lesbian and gay people)
0171-346 6807

Project for Advice, Counselling & Education (PACE)
0171-697 0014*

Rank Outsiders
(for serving and ex-armed forces personnel)
BCM Box 8431,
London WC1N 3XX
0171-652 6464*

Stonewall Housing Association
0171-359 5767*
Provides safe, shared accommodation for young lesbians and gay men aged between 17 and 25.
Also advice for those with accommodation problems.

Survivors
(for victims of male rape)
PO Box 2470,
London W2 1NW
0171-833 3737*
(Tues-Thurs 7-10pm)

Wales:
Internet website, for more information about Gay Wales:
http://www.mesmac-north-wales.org/resources

West and Wilde Lesbian and Gay Bookshop
25a Dundas Street
Edinburgh EH3
Mail order available.

(SEE ALSO NEXT PAGE)

YOUTH
Albert Kennedy Trust
for homeless lesbian and gay
teenagers
23 New Mount Street
Manchester M4 4DE
0161-953 4059 or
0171-831 6562*

National Freedom Youth
for under 26's
SAE: PO Box 72,
Middx HA5 2UJ

**North London Line Youth
Project**
Under 25's
Info: 0171-607 8346*

ETHNIC, RELIGIOUS AND
NON-RELIGIOUS
**Black Lesbian and Gay
Helpline**
0171-620 3885*

**Gay & Lesbian Humanist
Association (GALHA)**
(also provides commitment
ceremonies) 34 Spring Lane,
Kenilworth,Warks CV8 2HB
01926-858450

**Helpline for South East Asian
Lesbians and gays**
0171-837 7341* Th 8-10pm

**Jewish Gay and Lesbian
Group**
BM JGLG,
London WC1N 3XX
0181-905 3531*

**Lesbian & Gay Christian
Movement,** Oxford House,
Derbyshire Street,
London E2 6HG.
0171-739 1249*
Helpline 0171-739 8134*

Long Yang Club
(orientals and friends)
BCM/Wisdom,
WC1N 3XX
0181-311 5835*

Quest
Gay Catholic Group,
BM Box 2585,
London WC1N 3XX

Shakti
(South Asian L&G support)
PO Box 93,
28a Seymour Place,
London W1J 5WJ

EIRE
Dublin Gay Switchboard
(00 353 21) 872 1055

Gay Community News
monthly national newspaper
6 South William Street,
Dublin D2
00 353 1-671 0939

INTERNATIONAL
**International Gay & Lesbian
Association**
81 Rue de Marché au Charbon
B-1000 Brussels

ASSERTIVELY GAY
How to Build Gay Self-Esteem

Since its first publication, Assertively Gay has helped thousands of gay men achieve a happier life through the use of simple but effective assertiveness techniques.

Gay people are indoctrinated from an early age with the idea that their sexuality is sad, bad or hilarious. In adult life these negative feelings can lead to problems ranging from isolation to suicidal impulses. This book will help gay men understand where this uneasiness with their sexuality originates and how it can be turned into positive action for change.

- How assertiveness can help raise self-confidence
- Effective assertiveness techniques—and how to use them
- How to make creative improvements to your gay life
- Breaking out of the loneliness trap
- Successful coming out—using assertiveness to smooth the way
- Improve your sex life using assertiveness

"Over the last few months, Assertively Gay has helped me a great deal, allowing me to make choices about my sexuality that have transformed my life." — A.S. Gay Times.

"Speaks with a crystal clear voice, devoid of any pretension." - Our Times

"Top stuff!" - Boyz

£8. 95

A STRANGER IN THE FAMILY
How to Cope if your Child is Gay

As lesbians and gay men grow more confident in their sexuality, increasing numbers of them are "coming out" to their parents. All over the country, in thousands of homes, the news is being broken, "Mum, dad, I'm gay."

How can mothers and father deal with this shattering revelation? How will the family survive the news? Can they come to terms with the fact that a son or daughter or brother or sister is homosexual?

In this sympathetic and reassuring book, experienced counsellor Terry Sanderson guides worried parents through the stages of grief - from initial despair to complete acceptance. He provides the information, culled from authoritative sources, to enable them to make reasoned and constructive decisions about the future. He offers them the support and practical advice they need to get them through the crisis. This book also incudes a list of appropriate help agencies.

"Both reassuring and compassionate. And helpful not only for parents but their gay children, too." - Daily Mirror.

"Excellent. Packed with useful information." - Jane Butterworth, News of the World.

"Full of compassion and good sense, helpful information and telling case examples. It is an optimistic and life-affirming work." - Daniel O'Hara, GALHA Magazine.

£9. 95

A-Z OF GAY SEX
An Erotic Alphabet

In this erotic alphabet, Terry Sanderson tells you everything you ever wanted to know about gay sex - and then some more.

Encyclopaedic in scope, *The A-Z of Gay Sex* ranges from the how-to, where-to and who-with of man-to-man love. It gives you all the facts you need to ensure your sex life is happy, interesting—and safe.

From Abdomen to Zipper, Age to Youth—and all the great stuff in between—Terry Sanderson covers the nitty gritty of naughtiness in an entertaining and informative way.

- How does your sexual equipment work? It pays to know.
- Leather, rubber and other popular fetishes explored.
- Perversions—and how you can do them yourself.
- Worries about size—how big is big enough?
- Ever tried a double rub? Full details provided.
- New ideas for imaginative safer sex.
- The male multiple orgasm—and how to achieve it.

Terry Sanderson takes the guilt out of gay sex and presents it as a joyous, funny and extremely pleasant way to pass the time. The perfect book for bed-time dipping.

"Chirpy and sensible, full of common sense and fun." - Boyz

"The great thing about this book, apart from the fact that it is comprehensive, witty and sensible, is that even if you are not that way inclined, you will probably find out something useful and constructive about male sexuality." - Guardian.

£9. 95

THE POTTS PAPERS

"This hilarious book will make you laugh out loud," said *Thud* magazine about Terry Sanderson's comic and satiric new novel. Readers have complained that while engrossed in it they have embarrassed themselves with excessive guffawing on public transport. Now you can join in the fun with Doreen Potts and her crazy family.

- **Gary** - the gay son and his untrustworthy boyfriend, Bill. Doreen is doing her best to come to terms with her son's sexuality, but she can't quite get the hang of it.
- **Sylvia** - the man-mad daughter with a touch of religious mania. Now she's pregnant by the leader of a cult and on the run with his cash.
- **Iris** - the wily mother-in-law. What she doesn't know about swindling the DHSS isn't worth knowing. Is she going to come up with the right scheme to save the family from ruin?
- **Derek** - Doreen's long-suffering and depressive husband. Little does Doreen know that Derek's compulsive gambling is about to launch them on a roller-coaster ride that will lead to murder and, worse still, scandal in the tabloids.

"Packed with sex, gambling, random violence and a great deal of hoovering," Northwest Evening Mail

"The Potts Papers satirises religion, cheque-book journalism, snobbery, homophobia and family values... It may not be the book to give to your local vicar but give yourself a treat, buy it for yourself." - GM Humanist Magazine.

"Goes down like a delicious sorbet - a lemon sorbet, for this is a sharp dish... written with a constant, bubbling sense of humour." - New Humanist

"A gem" - The Rotherham Advertiser

£6. 95